AGAINST
THE STORM

by Masao Sugiura

First English edition published by Interventions Inc in 2019

Interventions is a not-for-profit, independent left wing book publisher. For further information:
www.interventions.org.au
interventionspublications@gmail.com
Trades Hall Suite 68
54 Victoria Street
Carlton VIC 3053

Originally published in Japan in 1964 as Senjichū Insatsu Rōdōsha no Tatakai no Kiroku (Record of the Struggle of Printworkers during the War). A second Japanese edition, published in 1981, was titled Wakamono wa arashi ni makenai: Senjika insatsu shuppan rōdōsha no teikō (Young people will not lose to the storm: the resistance of print and publishing workers during the war)

Author: Sugiura, Masao

Editor of English edition: Broadbent, Kaye
Translated by Kaye Broadbent and Mana Sato

Title of English edition: Against the storm: How Japanese printworkers resisted the military regime, 1935–1945

Design and layout by Viktoria Ivanova

ISBN: 978-0-9945378-5-0 : Paperback

© Japanese edition 1981 Masao Sugiura
© English edition 2019 Kaye Broadbent

The moral rights of the author have been asserted.
All rights reserved. Except as permitted under the Australian Copyright Act 1968 (for example, a fair dealing for the purposes of study, research, criticism or review), no part of this book may be reproduced, stored in a retrieval system, communicated or transmitted in any form or by any means without prior written permission.

All inquiries should be made to the editor of the English edition

All photos courtesy of Shuppanko Kurabu except where indicated.

A catalogue record for this book is available from the National Library of Australia

AGAINST THE STORM

How Japanese printworkers resisted the military regime, 1935–1945

By Masao Sugiura
Edited by Kaye Broadbent
Translated by Kaye Broadbent and Mana Sato

INTERVENTIONS
MELBOURNE

In memory of the members of the *Shuppankō Kurabu* (Print and Publishing Workers Club) and to activists everywhere fighting against oppression and building a better world.

Contents

	Preface	1
	Introduction	7
1	Facing the day of surrender from behind bars	17
2	The dark times	21
3	The sower of seeds – the preparatory period of the Club	27
4	Setback, and a new departure	31
5	Fighting the enemy trying to obstruct our organisation	39
6	Aiming for a connection with the greater masses	53
7	The unions heading to defeat through cooperation with the war	67
8	Keeping a low profile working among the masses	75
9	Destruction of the union movement and formation of the PIA	93
10	Difficulties we faced during the period of covert activity	109
11	Successive repression	115
12	The approaching defeat	123
13	Death of Shibata in prison and the defeat	131
14	The sown seeds bear fruit	139
	Afterword, February 1981	147
	Interview with Mr Masao Sugiura	151
	Glossary	157
	Bibliography	163

Preface

A lot of my research has been serendipitous and the catalyst for this book was no exception. In 2012, while researching sources for a chapter on resistance in Japan during World War 2, co-written with Tom O'Lincoln, I discovered a small treasure – *Senjichū Insatsu Rōdōsha no Tatakai no Kiroku* (*Record of the Struggle of Printworkers During the War*) in the labour library of the Ohara Social Research Institute, Hōsei University, Japan. The book detailing the formation and activity of the *Shuppankō Kurabu* (Print and Publishing Workers Club; hereafter called the Club) during Japan's war years was collated and printed by its surviving members in 1964 and privately distributed. Their aim was to commemorate their mentor and comrade, Shibata Ryūichirō (real name Shibata Ryūichi), who had died in prison months before emperor Hirohito's announcement in August 1945 that Japan had surrendered. Outlining his courage and persistence and demonstrating the esteem and admiration in which he was held by his comrades, the book was intended as a memento for Shibata's family.

From my research I knew that a number of Japan's unions belonged to the National Conference of Trade Unions (NCTU), the union federation created by the Japanese Communist Party. I believed that despite the heavy state repression meted out to left wing political activists and groups in the lead-up to and during the war years, there had to be more stories of union resistance. Until this time I had not come across any research or sources supporting that assumption. Finding this book was equivalent to winning the lottery.

With a view to bringing the story of the union and its members to light for an English speaking audience, I was eager to speak to those involved in the Club. Clearly, any surviving members would, if still living, be old or frail. I located a second version of the book – *Wakamono wa arashi ni makenai: Senjika insatsu shuppan rōdōsha no teikō (Young People Will Not Lose to the Storm: The resistance of print and publishing workers during the war)*. Published in 1981, it provides the basis for this translation

Early in 2016 I contacted a very well-read, knowledgeable, long-time friend and labour activist in Japan, Obata Yoshitake, who told me that the author, Masao Sugiura, was still alive and living near Tokyo. There are no adequate words to describe my euphoria on receiving this news. I was living an activist and researchers dream!

I arrived in Tokyo in May 2016. In spite of Mr Sugiura's age (he was almost 102 at the time of the interview), we talked for two hours. I left his home with a greater appreciation of the difficulties Japan's working population faced, and in particular the difficulties he and his comrades experienced in conducting union and left wing political activism during the war years. An edited version of the interview is included in the present edition.

....

In bringing this project to fruition, heartfelt thanks go to Masao Sugiura for allowing us to translate his book and for giving me his precious time. To him and his comrades and supporters for maintaining and developing a working class consciousness in the face of extraordinary state repression and torture. The history of that resistance provides future generations with a richer understanding of this period in world history. The history of the Club provides hope and inspiration and contributes to the tradition of struggle established by activists everywhere who have fought before us and who have paved the way for those of us fighting now.

I also want to thank the following: Obata Yoshitake for the initial introductions, which led to the meeting with Mr Sugiura, for sharing his knowledge of Japan's union movement, and his support and friendship over almost three decades; Obata Michiko for conversations on union activism that greatly enhanced my understanding; Terama Seiji for educating me on Japan's union movement and for the introductions that facilitated this aspect of union history coming to light; Hiroto Fujita for his permission to publish this history, for deeper explanations of historical aspects, for accompanying me on my visit to Mr Sugiura and for providing access to the photographic memorabilia; Yuki Hiroko for assistance in transcribing my interview with Mr Sugiura into written Japanese; Tom O'Lincoln and Janey Stone for encouraging me to continue this strand of research; Allen Myers who read over the manuscript and whose insightful questions and observations improved my explanations; and Viktoria Ivanova who designed the book layout. My thanks also to my comrades in Socialist Alternative for continuing to teach me so much about fighting for working class power, international solidarity with oppressed peoples, and about commitment to building a revolutionary organisation.

Due to the fire bombings on Tokyo and other places, there are very few photos and memorabilia remaining from the Club days. My thanks to Masao Sugiura and Hiroto Fujita for permission to include these images.

Translating this book had been a longstanding dream. A special thanks to Mana Sato, who assisted in the project and significantly improved the accuracy of the English translation.

In translating this work, we wanted as much as possible to convey the flavour and tone of the original text, so we have maintained much of the structure of the Japanese version but have made some editorial decisions to improve readability for an English speaking audience.

Following Japanese custom, the author used surnames to refer to people, except where there are two with the same name, in which case the personal name has also been used. In most cases the author omitted the conventional term of respect 'san'; we have followed his lead in this. We have used simplified English abbreviations for names of organisations, for example *Wakōkai* (the Japanese Language Materials Printworkers Society) is the Society, and *Shuppankō Kurabu* (the Print and Publishing Workers Club) is the Club. We have used diacritic marks to indicate long vowels, but have not used them on words familiar in English such as Tokyo or Yokohama. As the translators, we alone are responsible for any errors in translation.

Kaye Broadbent, Brisbane, February 2019

I would like to offer my biggest gratitude to Mr Sugiura for his lifelong activism and for this significant book. My heartfelt thanks to Kaye for inviting me to join this translation project. Being a Japanese who was born decades after the end of the Pacific War, I was not necessarily familiar with the details of events recounted in this volume. However, I do know very well of the fear of the reactionary trends which prompted Mr Sugiura to write this book. I would even dare say that today the fear is stronger and more real than ever. The ultra-right wing forces taking control in Japan are but the tip of the iceberg; indeed, the entire world seems to be full of strife and deepening rifts.

In this current world, Mr Sugiura's book is all the more relevant, not only because it tells us the concrete and admirable ways he and his comrades fought against an oppressive government, but also because it speaks of the universal spirit of resilience, of how we can open our eyes to reality and encourage ourselves to start moving forward, of how we can keep making our way forward with hope in our hearts. Of how, as Mr Sugiura so convincingly states, '[We] will not give into the storm'.

Mana Sato, Kyoto, February 2019

Introduction

The history of the *Shuppankō Kurabu* (the Print and Publishing Workers Club, hereafter the Club) is a fascinating insight into the times and difficulties facing Japan's working population, in particular left wing and union activists, during Japan's military build-up and the subsequent war (1931–45).[1] The story of the Club shows the tenacity and persistence of its members in first finding, and then developing, comrades in order to keep alive the embers of Japan's union movement and political activism in this dark and difficult period, while also sowing the seeds for the future. It reveals the stress and hardship they endured due to the constant pressure of evading heavy police repression and scrutiny. Those who were caught faced gaol and torture.

The actions of the ruling class and bourgeoisie in engaging in the project of militarisation are well known in the West. What is less well known are the actions of the working class in resisting this trajectory. Histories of the socialist and communist parties are available; however, the antiwar activities, strikes and other forms of resistance in factories central to the war effort are not as well documented. The story of the Club and its members is one element of the extraordinary resistance exhibited by Japan's working class.

---

1   I use the Fifteen Year War periodisation, which dates Japan's involvement in the war from the Manchurian Incident in September 1931 and ends with the surrender in August 1945; *see also* Banno 2014.

The main period covered by this book is that of Japan's increasing militarisation, particularly from the Marco Polo Bridge incident of 7 July 1937; it also references earlier periods, times when legislation had begun to place restrictions on the political and civil rights of the population.

In the Meiji period (1868–1912) Japan emerged from nearly 200 years of complete isolation. The Japanese ruling groups had entered a period of crisis that was only resolved after a series of struggles consolidated power and led to the return of the emperor as the symbolic head of state, with power concentrated in the hands of a clique of elder statesmen. Japan underwent an enormous political, social and economic transformation.

The first Sino–Japanese war (1894–95), a war of rivalry over the Korean peninsula, tested Japan's military strength. China's defeat resulted in Japan colonising the Korean peninsula. This region, together with Manchuria, became the focus of rivalry with Russia, with Japan increasing its influence in Manchuria and parts of Sakhalin.

The death of the Meiji emperor in 1912 led to the reign of his son who ruled under the name Taishō (1912–26). Historians consider the Taishō period one of relative peace and prosperity compared to the two decades that followed it. It was characterised by a relatively democratic but generally conservative government. The manufacturing sector doubled in growth, despite the devastating 1923 Kantō earthquake, which killed 150,000 people and destroyed most of the industrial capacity of Tokyo and Yokohama.

Japan's military expansion continued. Having fought on the side of the Allies in World War 1, Japan significantly expanded its reach by acquiring Germany's territories in China, Manchuria, Inner Mongolia and islands in the Pacific. It was part of the Allied invasion of Russia to fight the Red Army and remained in Russia until 1925. The emperor's son, Hirohito, had carried out official functions since his father's degeneration from a nervous breakdown in 1919; in 1926 the Taishō emperor died and the role formally passed to Hirohito who took the reign name Shōwa.[2]

The ruling parties' fear of discontent in the population, the growing influence of left wing ideas and the impact of social change led to the

---

2 Morris-Suzuki 1984: 3.

implementation of measures to prevent the spreading of dangerous thoughts. The Peace Preservation Law, for example, was introduced in 1925 and in 1928 was used after many left wing politicians were elected in that year. Most members of the small but expanding Japanese Communist Party (JCP), were rounded up and imprisoned.[3] As repression meted out to the population gathered in intensity, attacks on JCP members and sympathisers are of particular note. There was a series of mass arrests of 'reds', murders and torture of left wing activists in 1922, 1928 and April 1929. On 15 March 1928 in one day 'over 1200 communists and sympathisers were arrested and in 1929, 700 more. The persecution of communists continued into the 1930s.'[4] In October 1932 nearly 1500 activists were arrested nationally. Newspapers carried numerous reports of unexplained deaths in police custody.

The cases of Iwata Yoshimichi and Kobayashi Takiji are the most high profile and are worth elaborating. They are mentioned by name in the book, and their experiences confirm that the torture endured by Sugiura, Taguchi and Shibata while imprisoned was fairly standard procedure for the Special Police. Iwata Yoshimichi was a member of the central committee of the JCP. His death on 13 November 1932 was particularly sensational, as was the cover up that ensued. Although officials stated that the cause was a combination of beriberi and heart disease, an autopsy found no evidence of these conditions, but rather evidence of massive internal bleeding and a swollen chest and thighs. Iwata's parents demanded an investigation into how the death occurred and named several police investigators and the head of the Special Police as implicated in their son's death. However, under pressure from the Tokyo District Court, the parents dropped their demands. Kobayashi Takiji was a well-known author of proletarian literature, including *The Crab Cannery Ship (Kani Kōsen)*. He joined the party in 1931 and was arrested and tortured many times. He died on 20 February 1933 from horrific injuries consistent with torture.[5]

---

3   Morris-Suzuki 1984: 6.
4   Hane 2000: 123.
5   Information from Mitchell 1992: 82–3.

This increased domestic control over the population and ever tighter repression was associated with increased militarisation. In 1929 one military leader wrote: 'Japan must expand overseas to achieve political stability at home.'[6] In the early 1930s, participants at cabinet meetings repeatedly complained that domestic unrest was a 'great problem, impeding national defence'.[7]

In the Manchurian Incident (1931), Japan seized three of China's northern provinces and turned them into the puppet state Manchukuo, which it officially recognised in September 1932.

The struggle between military and civilian rule intensified further in the middle of the decade. On 26 February 1936 a group of young army officers staged a *coup d'état* with the stated aim of ridding the Japanese government of 'evil' on behalf of the emperor. There were about 1500 in the rebel army compared to 14,000 remaining on the side of the government.[8] The impact of the coup was far-reaching; the government tightened restrictions on civilian political activity and used the coup as a pretext for banning May Day activities in 1936.[9] The government-controlled labour front, the Patriotic Industrial Association (PIA), was established for full-time workers in 1940 with a separate organisation created for non-permanent workers. Here, the government and employers saw the enterprise as one family. The police, with the collaboration of right wing labour leaders, organised and supervised the PIA and organised every workshop with the objective of compelling workers to submit unconditionally to forced labour, overwork and low wages.

Ruling class actions in this period did not go unchallenged as the period was marked by social upheaval and resistance.[10] The ideas of socialism came to Japan in the Meiji period. Demands for universal male suffrage (won in 1925), social welfare and workers' rights were key. Socialists

---

6 Ienaga 1979: 11.
7 Gordon 1991: 265.
8 Banno 2014: 217.
9 Shioda 1982: 119.
10 This section draws on Broadbent and O'Lincoln 2015.

worked to build a movement against the Russo–Japanese war, arguing in their newspaper that 'war benefits the bourgeoisie but sacrifices the common people'.[11] Disenchantment with the political system, inflation and austerity policies and limited civil liberties prompted protests, particularly by students, workers, peasants and minority groups. The Japan Socialist Party formed in 1906, the JCP in 1922 and the General Federation of Labour (GFL) in 1919. The *Suiheisen* (the Levellers Association) was set up in 1922 to address the demands of the *burakujūmin* (outcast people) who are ethnically Japanese but are discriminated against as in the past they largely undertook tasks such as slaughtering animals or tanning hides, defined as unclean in Buddhism. All the new organisations attempted to address the widespread anger and hostility to the ruling parties. The GFL was Japan's largest union federation and, while it condemned Japan's attack on the Russian Revolution in 1918 and called for self-government in Korea, it did not maintain its radicalism.

In the atmosphere of the 1920s, left wing culture coalesced and became the basis for criticism of the growing militarism. Continued repression destroyed many social, political and cultural outlets but circles in factories and villages enabled workers and peasants to develop their own independent culture. These groups also later enabled the illegal JCP to operate above ground where it played a major role in the mass dissemination of antiwar, Marxist and revolutionary ideas.[12]

The history of the Club covered in this book shows us how these activities were carried out. Importantly, it deepens our understanding of the devastating impact of the war on the population and contributes to a developing body of literature[13] revealing the extent and nature of resistance by the Japanese population to the government's drive to war. This history serves as an important counterweight to the belief that Japan's union movement cooperated thoroughly in the repression of workers by the state or else completely disappeared.

---

11   Ienaga 1979: 13–14.
12   Broadbent and O'Lincoln 2015: 297.
13   See, for example, Dower 1993.

Unionisation rates during the war time period were quite low, 5 per cent. Nonetheless it was a period of intense industrial activity. The number of strikes reached 2456 in 1931 and, while dropping in the intervening years, reached 2126 in 1937 when 231,622 workers participated in strikes.[14] In March 1932 under the leadership of the NCTU, the Tokyo subway workers strike successfully demanded improvements in workers' conditions. The impact of this success was widespread. It is in this context that the Tokyo Printing Company and Yasuhisa strikes of 1935 mentioned in the book took place; Club members were active in their support.

Elements of Japan's union movement during the 1930s were active in opposing the war and growing militarism but by 1937 many of the representative trade unions had limited their industrial action and virtually stopped functioning as trade unions. Illegal unions were also suppressed at this time. From 1931 the GFL's union contracts began incorporating a promise of 'industrial service to the nation'.[15] By July 1940 the GFL had dissolved as had most of the remaining non-federation affiliated unions.

Nonetheless, a number of important industrial disputes occurred in military industries, even after the dissolution of the union movement. Nationally, many struggles broke out due to workers' heightened class consciousness and their resistance to the war.[16] In 1942, for example, communists organised and led action in a steelworks controlled by the navy, with workers demanding improved pay and working conditions. They protested by sabotaging production, including by deliberately producing rejects. A similar sabotage action was carried out by workers in the Hitachi company's factory in Kameido, a working class area of Tokyo, to try to force management to agree to their demands for higher wages.[17]

The book begins with Japan's surrender in 1945 and the occupation of Japan by US and other Allied forces. The occupation was supposed to

---

14 Information on the Japanese trade union movement is from Broadbent and O'Lincoln 2015: 299–301 unless otherwise specified.

15 Gordon 1991: 299.

16 Ohara Social Science Institute 1965: 18.

17 Fujihara 1975: 208-10; 293-94

be humanitarian, to foster democracy and work for peace. In practice it was racist, vindictive, favoured the rich and began rearmament. General Douglas MacArthur, commander of US army forces in the Far East, ordered no fraternisation with or feeding the Japanese although many were starving. Western attempts to reform Japan became half-hearted when fighting communism in China and Korea soon became a priority. Those collaborators who might have been purged at the end of the war were now allies against communism so leftists were hounded instead. As Thomas A. Bisson, who worked for the occupation authorities, wrote in his diary: 'The one really significant challenge to the old guard Japanese establishment has been turned back.'[18]

The working class quickly understood that it had to rely on its own activism and could not look to the Occupation forces for assistance. The Japanese ruling class had been smashed in the war, so now a space opened up for working class struggle. Interest in trade unionism and industrial militancy exploded in the post-war period. Total union membership in late 1945 was 600,000, rising to 6.7 million or 53 per cent of the workforce by June 1948.[19] Protests over food culminated in the Food May Day demonstrations of 1946. The protest attracted about 2 million workers, half a million in Tokyo alone. Chairman of the JCP Tokuda Kyūichi drew prolonged cheers when he shouted 'Down with the emperor!' The day was filled, one observer wrote, 'with a curious kind of joy – perhaps the kind of luminous joy a prisoner of war feels on regaining freedom'.[20]

This book is part of the history of class struggle in Japan and shows that working people will strike, struggle and organise even under the most repressive of political conditions. But their persistence in opposing the military regime came at an enormous personal cost.

The overwhelming determination of Sugiura and many other activists to keep union traditions alive in Japan during the period of militarism bore fruit very early in the post-war period and many Club members were at the

---

18 Finn 1992: 141
19 Nimura 1994: 67
20 Moore 1983: 177-178

centre of this activity. The story described in this book unfolded against the background of increasing militarism and repression of trade union activity. The book was written to disprove the assertion that there were no trade unions in Japan during the war period. Sugiura describes the activities of the print and publishing workers in establishing the Society of Japanese Language Materials Printworkers (the Society) in 1935 after the Tokyo printworkers strike in order to represent the interests of rank and file workers. Subsequently, the Society changed its basis of operation and in 1937 converted to the Print and Publishing Workers Club (the Club) in order to maintain contact between workers in whatever way was still possible. In doing so, Sugiura and his comrades faced danger, prison and torture, but as he himself says:

> We did what would be just a normal thing for any trade unionist to do ... While all of Japan's trade unions were destroyed under the repression of war time fascism, the Club defended its organisation, saving the thread from eradication that would later bring about the Print and Publishing union.

The Club's achievements and those of Shibata Ryūichirō and Shiraishi Mitsuo are now remembered with a commemorative stone, which was erected on 6 November 1977, at Jogan Temple in Katsushika, a working class area of Tokyo. The location is symbolic, as the temple is close to an area where Shibata and Shiraishi lived for many years. The calligraphic inscription was provided by the then chairman of the JCP Nosaka Sanzō.

Sugiura wrote the first edition of this book in 1964 to honour the memory of Shibata and preserve the memory of Japan's union activism during the war. *Senjichū Insatsu Rōdōsha no Tatakai no Kiroku (Record of the Struggle of Printworkers during the War)* drew on the assistance and recollections of the surviving 32 former members of the Club[21]. The second edition *Wakamono wa arashi ni makenai: Senjika insatsu shuppan rōdōsha no teikō (Young People Will Not Lose to the Storm: The resistance of print*

---

21 The number quoted in the book although in the interview Masao Sugiura mentions thirty six people were involved.

and publishing workers during the war) was published in 1981 to educate young union activists in the history of workers' resistance and encourage others to become active.

Masao Sugiura notes that while there were people who participated in the Club's activities who were class conscious, there were also many who were simply supporters and that many died during the struggle. He also acknowledges that these people are not forgotten. Publishing this book in English is one way of ensuring that knowledge of their courage, conviction and activism in the face of repression reaches a broader audience.

Kaye Broadbent, Brisbane, February 2019

1
Facing the day of surrender from behind bars

I greeted 15 August 1945, the day of Japan's surrender, from a solitary cell in Yokohama prison. The atmosphere of the whole prison that morning was unusual, as there had been no warden's voice calling us to get up. I ate the substandard meal that was delivered and got ready for work, but the materials for doing the job did not come. The warden also did not come around and the area around the cell was eerily quiet. After I had eaten lunch, I wondered why no-one had come around. From downstairs a sonorous recitation was audible. When I looked out through the peephole the jack of all trades trustee, a prisoner who assisted the wardens, was reciting a poem in a sad voice. This man was, as rumour had it, a right wing fighter who had tried to assassinate a financier and had been imprisoned for attempted murder. I thought his singing was strange. Usually, if we sang in a loud voice, we were beaten up by the warden. While I was looking out at this scene, there was a signal from the cell opposite mine.

In these cells, prisoners who had had their punishments decided but who had not yet been sent to the factory, were housed for four to five days. It was a small room with about three people at any one time. Someone signalled to me from one of these cells. When I opened my food slot, they also had their food slot open and were writing something in the air. After they had written a letter they would nod to ask if I understood. When I nodded back, they would write the next letter. When I did not understand, I would shake my head from side to side and they would rewrite the letter.

What I deciphered was 'Japan lost the war'. I knew that Japan's situation in the war had deteriorated, but to lose! Everything became clear. I bowed deeply and thanked the person in the cell opposite me.

I heard the next day, by the writing in the air method, that the emperor had broadcast his surrender speech. After shutting the food slot, I started to consider how this would affect us prisoners. I thought we would be released soon. On the other hand, the warden had been saying crazy things like: 'If we lose the war, we will get rid of you and then we will die.' We had no choice but to trust the course of events.

However, we were not released, nor were we killed: we political prisoners remained locked up until 6 October. According to what I found out later, the powerful in Japan didn't want to release political prisoners, and thus prevented our immediate acquittal.

Becoming criminals under bad laws

On 6 October materials for doing my job did not arrive, so I spent the day in my cell, just eating and lounging about. When the day was almost over, the sound of a key opening cell doors got closer. While I was wondering if it was a cell inspection, my cell door opened. The warden told me to grab all my things and get out. I wondered if I was being transferred. I had resigned myself to prison, so it did not immediately occur to me that I was being released. I snatched my personal effects and left my cell. Outside, when I started to descend to the lower floor, we were told to form a line. I saw my comrade Taguchi. We obeyed the warden's directions and exited the cell area. Under millions of stars, we followed the warden's directions and walked down the long walkway we had passed through at the time of our imprisonment towards the church where the prison governor and chaplain were waiting. The governor, standing before us, began to speak to us in a tone more polite than usual.

> Until now, you were kept in here for disrupting the public peace.
> As you know, Japan lost and the war is over. You are now no longer criminals. From today you are to go home. Even though our points

of view have differed so far, from now on we must work together and overcome this difficult period in Japan. Please do not think badly of me.

He spoke thus and looked at the face of the chaplain. Hearing the governor's words, an angry roar rose up from the political prisoners.

'What are you saying? Now you are saying we are not criminals! Cut the crap. Who is taking responsibility for the fact that we were locked up in here for years? Stop kidding around. Arseholes!'

Gnashing their teeth, some tried to launch themselves at the governor. Others responded with 'Wait, wait, hang on a minute. We do not know the circumstances from the governor's speech alone. Let's just get out of here right now. You can argue all you want later.'

Laws are a frightening thing. Until yesterday, we were criminals under the Peace Preservation Law [PPL 1925–45] created by the imperial government, and because of this, we had been imprisoned for many years. But now, these laws had been abolished by order of the Allied army, and from today we were not criminals. Thus, we were released.

Why was I imprisoned in Yokohama gaol for three years? Why did I have to face the tragedy of my close comrade dying in prison? Why did my wife, in my absence, have to suffer the cruel fate of being burned to death in the massive bombing attack on Tokyo on 10 March 1945, leaving our young daughter behind? These were all because we did what would be just a normal thing for any trade unionist to do today.

At the time the Club was organising, the printing industry was largely a non-union workforce. Unemployment was high and workers had no rights. Naturally, we tried to unionise by ourselves, to protect our occupation and jobs as well as our livelihoods. Through unionising, we also tried to satisfy our interest in cultural pursuits; we organised study groups to further our knowledge, working together to improve ourselves. But because we were doing these most natural things under the worst law of the century, the PPL, we were criminalised and imprisoned.

Japan had invaded China but had met resistance from the Chinese people, and was now bogged down in the war and could neither advance nor retreat. Japan's rulers, including the military, had taken a huge gamble in waging a war with the US and England, using it as an opportunity to try to force them into peace. They smashed all progressive political parties and trade unions and created the state-sponsored organisations the Imperial Rule Assistance Association (IRAA) and the Patriotic Industrial Association (PIA). The government brought Japan's workers into the war. Those political parties and trade unions that opposed the military course were suppressed and then annihilated, leaving only those political parties and trade unions who supported the government's war policies. Those who surrendered to the government's threats, agreed one by one to disband their organisations. As a result, they sold out the workers and the working population to the government and the army. The Club opposed this direction. But if we had opposed the direction openly, we would have all been arrested. With no other choice, and in the presence of the Special Police and the like, we performed a fake dissolution ceremony, and then continued our activism covertly. The Special Police punished us for our actions with arrest and imprisonment.

It is said that Japan's entire union movement during the war years was forced to disband and was reduced to zero. Looking back, though, during that darkest war period, we can see that the print and publishing industry union movement continued, preventing the organisation of workers from completely disappearing.

I will tell you about the path that Japan's union movement pursued during that darkest period, how we were made to surrender in front of the army and ruling class, and how, even during the dark repressive period, a small group of workers continued to fight, regardless of the risks.

What did the movement that existed during this repression look like? I want to tell you the story based on the circumstances of the time and the path we took.

2
The dark times

The fateful meeting with our mentor, Shibata Ryūichirō

'You're Sugiura?'

I was picking type[22] at work when a male voice called out, 'I'm Shibata Ryūichirō'. The caller was tall, with fair skin, reddish brown hair in a close cropped style and wearing very thick glasses – he looked rather like a Buddhist monk. I thought: Ah, so this is him. Two or three nights earlier, when I met my friend Shibata Ichirō, he told me 'There's a typesetter employed as a temporary worker in your company called Shibata Ryūichirō who said he would come around to your work area to meet you'. We exchanged greetings and after agreeing to meet up later, he acted as though he had come on another errand and then returned to his work area.

We both worked at Tokyo Printing, located in the Tokyo working class suburb of Fukagawa. The company occupied several small buildings, with three larger buildings, which comprised the office, print works and book printing section, as the core. The type printing section I worked in was housed in a wooden building 30 × 15 metres. The book printing section occupied half, while the type picking area occupied the other half. About 80 workers worked in the building and Shibata Ryūichirō [called simply

---

22 Selecting *kanji* or logographic Chinese characters used in printing the Japanese language.

Shibata in this book] had come from the book printing section of the building. This was the first time I had met him. From this time on, Shibata completely changed my destiny. He is the reason I persisted in the union movement until my retirement. I do not regret it at all. Thanks to Shibata I think I have lived a very full life.

My background

I lived in Fukagawa with both parents, two brothers and seven sisters. My father, employed on a delivery boat working up and down the nearby Sumida river for a sugar company, was the sole provider for the family. It was a life of extreme poverty. My father went too far in trying to fulfil his dream of owning our own house. He borrowed money from a loan shark and bought a small wooden house. Then, although we couldn't afford it, he employed a carpenter at enormous expense to build a second floor. Having to repay the loan shark made the family budget even tighter. My older siblings went to work as soon as they completed primary school in order to supplement the family income. One of my older brothers went to work in a small printing factory, constantly working overtime with no day off. As a result he contracted tuberculosis and was regularly treated in a clinic, which made the family budget even tighter. All of us at home were undernourished and our health suffered. A small mercy was that, with the assistance of a friend of my father, I was taken on as an apprentice at the nearby Tokyo Printing, one of Tokyo's largest print works.

The economy at the time was depressed. At Tokyo Printing wages were low and to supplement them everyone did overtime. Only the first and third Sundays were days off. Workers all lived in the shabbiest houses. With few pleasures, at lunchtime people played cards, losing what little money they had. On pay day many visited the local red light district.

My biggest concern at this time was whether to quit the company. In 1933 I was 20 years old, had completed my conscription examination and I felt I was good enough to be treated as a fully-fledged worker. I was conceited and in a casual manner would challenge the temporary workers to competitions, putting them under pressure while preening myself, which was a rather mean thing to do. But, as an apprentice my daily wages were low – only 80 sen.[23] If I had gone to a different company as a qualified type picker I could earn between 1 yen 80 sen and 2 yen. So I wanted to quit and go elsewhere, but because the economy was depressed, there were few permanent positions available. If I left I would have been employed as a temporary worker and have to move around to different workshops looking for work. The wages at my present company were low but at least I could work every day. As a temporary worker, it would be good when I had work but I would be partially unemployed. I understood that much and so could not bring myself to leave.

The youth of the 1930s

In 1933, many people were unemployed. All industries were similar to the print industry. It was a time of gloom. I remember the commercial newspaper ran a current affairs cartoon showing a young person carrying a backpack who was at a crossroads. He was thinking about which path to take. There were three roads drawn in front him – one was the road to suicide, another was the road to decadence and the third was the road to Marxism. As depicted in this cartoon, suicide was popular, with several high profile incidences reported in the newspapers. Most young people chose the path of decadence – alcohol, gambling and philandering.

If you wished to live as an earnest human being, there was no other path but to fight, to follow the doctrine of Marxism. Today the socialist and communist movements are legal, but at the time, under the imperial government, they were prohibited. The reach of the Special Police extended throughout the country and the PPL was the weapon used to suppress socialists and communists. In order to isolate the mass of the working population from them, the Special Police directed the media to make those arrested look worse than the most heinous of criminals, making people fearful of them. From the mid-1920s, Japanese Communist Party (JCP)

---

23   100 sen = 1 yen; 80 sen is around $A5.60 in today's money.

members and other socialists and democrats began to be arrested. When newspapers reported on these arrests, the journalists used photos showing them with messy hair and an evil look, so that ordinary people had the worst impression of them.

In my workplace, there were two or three young people who were rumoured to be political. From time to time one of them would bring tickets for the Tsukiji Small Theatre, which he sold to us for 30 sen. I bought these tickets once or twice and was surprised to learn what the atmosphere was like.

I can still remember the smell of the delicious pork cutlets coming from the restaurant that reached my nose when I sat in the theatre seat. The corridor was a dramatic sight. Several cops wearing helmets and sabres were present and during the performance they would leave their torches on and observe the audience. The lights would go down and the theatre would darken, and then, from somewhere, a voice would sing the *Internationale*. The police would fly over in the direction of the singer and yell 'Hey, don't sing that'. Then, from the other side, someone else would start singing the *Internationale*, and then the cops would head in that direction to make them stop. People would yell 'Go! Go!' in encouragement and when the noise died down, a lively performance of a worker's strike would unfold on stage. The audience would get excited when the actor playing a corrupt leader entered the stage. They would warn in loud voices 'He's corrupt, don't be fooled'. When the strike ended in defeat, the red flag was unfurled on stage and several worker heroes demonstrating on stage would scream at the top of their lungs that they would fight to the end. The audience stood and applauded them enthusiastically.

When the play ended and we left fully satisfied, someone would be handing out leaflets to the departing crowd. In no time at all the plain clothes cops, who were undercover among the audience, would rush out to arrest them. The departing theatre audience tried to prevent this. Watching all the commotion unfold I left for home feeling it was very scary.

On the day after, hearing that I had been to the theatre, a guy in my workplace who was known to be political came over and said, 'How was it? Last night was great, wasn't it?' Those in my workplace known to be political however, weren't really oriented to workers and did not regularly carry out actions in the interests of the workers. For that reason, they were not trusted by the majority in the workplace and were isolated. Workers like us, despite being raised in poverty, at that time did not have an interest in class war; and so the majority of us tended to avoid these people. In response, they regarded us with scorn, saying things like 'His [class] consciousness is low'.

With my impoverished household environment and a workplace with no hope or dreams to look forward to, my mood at this time was grey and despairing. Right at this time, Shibata Ryūichirō appeared. He was a member of the National Confederation of Trade Unions (NCTU), which had recently been infiltrated by a spy in Tokyo. I heard that Shibata was on the committee investigating this incident. But I do not know if he was a member of the communist party. In later years, when several members of the Club leadership were arrested, the very first thing the Special Police asked was whether we were involved in terrorist activities and whether Shibata was a member of the communist party. But we did not know, and finally the Special Police gave up. But in the story I am about to tell, it will be confirmed that he was a communist.

3
The sower of seeds – the preparatory period of the Club

Strengthening the wartime structure

Shibata visited my workshop in 1934. The mainstream daily newspapers were filled with articles on Japan's creation of Manchukuo, with the government-appointed puppet Pu Yi as emperor. Because of the success of the Manchurian invasion, domestic militarisation was growing stronger. This did not solve the absurdity of Japanese capitalism. The ruling class was preparing to launch an even greater invasion on the Chinese mainland.

The Manchurian Incident stimulated production in the military industries while the peacetime industries continued to be depressed, especially the printing industry. This was due to the large companies putting the smaller print works under pressure. They engaged in price dumping, forcing smaller companies into bankruptcy. The large companies also forced the government to create the Industry Control Law and the Factory Union Law in order to regulate smaller companies.

The smaller companies themselves transferred the entire burden onto the workers. They introduced the temporary employment system throughout the industry, which meant printworkers could be sacked at any time. This system was not like the long-term employment that exists now. Workers were employed for three days or a week; for a temporary worker a month was considered a long time. This system drove the majority of printworkers into a state of semi unemployment. In addition, with inflation, prices of commodities skyrocketed; as a result, the lives of printworkers became more and more difficult.

Creating a literary circle

In these circumstances printworkers tended to fall into a state of despair. But on the other hand, these were conditions that could make printworkers stand up and fight. Because of his experience as a temporary worker Shibata started to think about creating an organisation of printworkers. The first person he took as a comrade was Sakamura, who loved literature and who worked nearby as a typesetter. Both lived in Tateishi. From a chance meeting they soon became very close friends and comrades. Next, Shibata met Shiraishi, who also lived in Tateishi. These young men were the core who created the circle called *Godō* [Chinese umbrella tree] and they published a literary magazine of the same name. But this circle never went beyond gathering lovers of literature. Also, because it was rather exclusive as a discussion group, members started to have doubts about it. They started to think that they had to create a group which was based on workers.

Shibata at that time frequently went to work at a print works in Fukagawa as a temporary worker. There he got to know Shibata Ichirō. Since Shibata, Itamura and Shiraishi wanted to create a magazine for like-minded people, Shibata Ichirō actively encouraged them and gave advice. He oversaw the process, from collecting the manuscripts and editing, to the delivery, and helped these young men, who were grappling with producing a magazine for the first time.

The publication of *Ayumi*

The magazine was not aimed at literary people but at workers. Shibata wanted the magazine to be one that workers could feel free to submit an item to without feeling ashamed of their ability; they eventually welcomed this stance. The core group of workers soon grasped that in this way the magazine was a tool in the organisation of workers.

The magazine was named *Ayumi* [path, or step]. On the first page was a preface with a sentimental poem and after that there were poems by women workers and *haiku*, which were popular among printworkers at the time, especially type pickers and typesetters. *Ayumi* was bought by workmates of members of the circle, and by workers in different factories. Ten copies found their way to Tokyo Printing. Others were bought by workers in the Shiba district, which, at the time, was the main location for small and medium sized print workshops.

The editors included, among others, Shibata Ichirō and Shibata Ryūichirō. As a result of their friendship with the owner of a small print works, they were given access to the facilities there and together, with the cooperation of a group of workers, they picked and set the type to print the magazine outside of work hours.

Many young workers, in assisting with the production of *Ayumi*, were nurtured and became the nucleus in the formation of the Shiba branch of what would become the Club.

The success of the first issue of *Ayumi* encouraged the participants; the second and third issues soon followed. Copies of all the issues found their way into numerous workplaces.

The establishment of the magazine soon had a good outcome. Shibata, Shiraishi and Shibata Ichirō, who had been temporary workers, were soon able to get work at Tokyo Printing, although only as temporary workers. This result was achieved through the positive endorsement of *Ayumi*'s readers. Tokyo Printing, a large company, employed many young workers whom Shibata was keen to organise. As I was employed in the same company, Shibata also approached me. Later Shibata became one of the temporary workers who regularly came to work at Tokyo Printing.

4
Setback, and a new departure

Strike at Tokyo Printing

In 1935, inflation had a devastating effect on industry. In the peacetime industries such as printing, there was no work and the situation was dire. While commodity prices were increasing, wages were not. In fact the value of real wages was decreasing daily.

In Tokyo Printing, there was talk among a group of comparatively progressive young men of the need to raise wages or they would not be able to survive. Some of the workers at Tokyo Printing belonged to the Kantō [Tokyo and surrounds] Publishers Union. But the union did not take up, push or organise around the serious demands of the young workers, so they decided that they would have to push their own demands and organise and fight by themselves.

If their demands could be taken up, it was clear the struggle would develop. Shibata and Shiraishi gathered the more politically advanced workers and started to organise the struggle through their demand to raise wages. This soon spread to many other workplaces.

When it was clear the Kantō Publishers Union had no choice but to take up the demands of its members, it put forward a strong demand to increase the average wage from 98 sen to one yen. The company's response however, turned the tables on their demands. They proposed to raise the wages of only a selection of employees, with the remaining employees either having their wages pegged or even reduced. On top of that, the company proposed sacking all 20 of the highest earning employees – those who were paid over two yen. Clearly this proposal was an attack aimed at all employees. Two hundred and twenty workers saw the threat of sackings as personal and so with demands including opposition to sackings and pay increases, they went on indefinite strike on 21 March 1935. Predictably the company locked out the workers the same day. In addition, to undermine the union, the company hired thugs to guard the factory and had police escort the scabs into the factory to continue working.

The strike committee rented a space in the district of Fukagawa, set up its headquarters and prepared for a long struggle.

The strike committee put up posters around the factory and the boss's house. They approached friendly organisations to win support, they picketed outside the factory and tried to win over the scabs.

During the strike Shibata and Shiraishi officially acted as though they had no role in it, but the young people who were to form the centre of the struggle gathered around the two straight away. The real strike leadership occurred around Shibata in a covert form. Every night a meeting was held to decide strategy. The role of the group around *Ayumi* not only led the strike from day to day, but also through the strike developed a new layer of leaders. Once the day's activities had ended, the activists would gather until late evening. They developed their consciousness through studying texts such as Lenin's *What is to be done?*. Through the strike, they came to understand the natural development of trade union activism and the central responsibility of their leadership role. The young people were filled with courage to know that they themselves were the hidden leadership of the strike, and that the victory or defeat of the strike was down to their efforts. In reflecting on that time Shiraishi said: 'The pressure got worse and I became dejected, as the indications that we would be defeated were increased.' Shibata said:

> If you look at the prognosis for the strike, I think it is unlikely that we will win. But we cannot throw it in. The thing we need to think about is that even if wages were increased or the sackings were overturned,

these are no more than short-term wins and would not constitute a definitive victory for the working class. There is no need for us to be swayed by economic victories or defeats. From my viewpoint, what is important is the number of class conscious activists who will emerge from this struggle to actively join the class struggle. Let us grasp this firmly and lead the struggle.

Fundraising activity of the federation of 35 companies

The group around *Ayumi* formed not only the inner core of the strike committee but also were central to gathering external support and fundraising for strikes, starting with the Tokyo Printing strike.

Several workers, including Sakamura, who were involved in the publishing of *Ayumi*, created the Support Group for the Workers Opposing the Dismissals at Tokyo Printing. Although I had left Tokyo Printing by then, I was included in this activity. We would divide up the local area and visit all the neighbouring print shops. I still remember how under Sakamura's guidance we would discuss the issue with non-union workers.

We would visit a factory, meet with the workers, explain the strike situation and then collect five or ten sen each which accumulated into a rather impressive sum. From those workers we received introductions to other workplaces which then broadened our network. Eventually, individual workers from over 35 print workshops donated to the support fund. Normally that money would have been delivered to the strike headquarters right away but Sakamura, before delivering the money, revisited those who had donated and said 'Thanks to all of you we managed to gather donations from 35 companies. I want to take this to strike headquarters without delay, but instead of giving individual names, I think it would give the striking workers greater strength to know that there were supporters from 35 companies. Is it alright if I represent you as part of the federation?' He received their consent and representatives were selected from the workers in the 35 companies who had donated the funds and they were asked to deliver the money.

On delivering the donations, the representatives would pass on their greetings. After this they would visit all the workplaces and report on the proceedings. Through this process supporters from the companies would become linked and with Sakamura at the centre, a cooperative organisation of activists developed.

In participating in the fundraising activity, I slowly began to grasp how important it was for the working class to support each other and that however, small my efforts were, they constituted a significant part of the work of creating solidarity among the working class.

The strike bogs down

The Tokyo Printing strike appeared to have become bogged down. Every day scabs ostentatiously entered the factory under police escort. Although it was only partial, the operations in the workshop encouraged the company to feel confident. The boss declared he would not give in, and was even prepared to dissolve the company in order to smash the strike committee. For this reason the strike became bogged down which created a mix of optimism and pessimism. At one time there was coercive intervention by the police due to the fact that Pu Yi, Japan's puppet from the Manchurian empire, was invited to Japan under the protection of the combined squadron led by the warship *Hiei*.

The police had stood with the capitalists to prolong the Tokyo Printing strike, but now they changed their attitude and all of a sudden turned to mediation. They made it look as if they wanted to settle the dispute for the workers' benefit. Their real feeling, however, was that it would be inconvenient if one section of Tokyo was engaged in violent struggle at the time of the Manchurian emperor's visit to Japan. Their idea was to settle the strike completely before Pu Yi arrived, but the proposed conditions of settlement were completely unacceptable to the strike committee. The mediation ended badly and there seemed to be no idea as to when the strike might be resolved. Then, one morning something occurred that led to an abrupt defeat.

A young man from the strike committee was at the picket line when a scab, who had previously entered the workplace in a truck under police escort, walked in. The young striker tried to persuade the scab, but he refused to listen. The scab's rude response upset the striker and he pushed the man over. He should not have done this. The scab hit his head and went home, where he later died.

The police jumped at this opportunity and carried out a general arrest of the strike committee.

Thus the Tokyo Printing strike, which had continued for over 100 days, ended in total defeat. All that remained was to get the company to recognise the conditions of capitulation, which included rehiring seventy workers from among those who had been sacked. Soon after the strike ended, one officer from the Special Police, Matsumura, who had been a constant ally of the company during the strike, was taken on by the company as the head of security, which exposed the unity between the company and the police. This was how the Tokyo Printing strike was resolved.

It is essential, however, to understand why the strike turned violent.

The power of the imperial system was extreme beyond anything today. Workers and farmers were oppressed. The NCTU, the militant union, had debated whether to include the overthrow of the imperial system in its policy platform. In that debate, in order to reveal the reality of the imperial system, one member noted:

> Japan's imperial system is a remnant of feudal, despotic politics. The imperial system is a machinery of exploitation, armed from head to toe. If workers and farmers try to put their daily economic demands to the capitalist landlords and fight, however small the demands are, as the struggle intensifies – which means the more acute their immediate demands are, they would collide with the imperial government authorities. Workers and farmers, the vast majority of the country's citizens who are referred to as the emperor's 'babies', are putting their acute demands for bread to their employer and negotiating. Despite this, the imperial authorities would trample over the workers' and farmers' demands while taking up swords to protect the capitalist landlords. This is what we

experience as the usual state.[24]

The imperial police of the time questioned citizens whenever they felt like it, and conducted searches of their person or personal effects without search warrants. They also committed cruel acts, including arrests, torture and imprisonment. I would say they were acting much worse than the fascist regime of South Korea in 1981.

Under such conditions, when there were strikes, the police were always on the side of the company and suppressed workers, grasping the smallest of opportunities to attack them. If workers presented a list of demands to the company and pressured it to negotiate, they would be arrested. If protests occurred in the workplace, it was raided and workers would be arrested. If they resisted even a little, they would be arrested for disturbing the peace. When the strike committee, in the name of solidarity, tried to convince members to join in, the police would claim the committee abducted, captured, or threatened this individual, using it as a pretext to interfere.

In this way, with the enemy overwhelmingly stronger, and supporters weak, the working class tended to feel impatient. Becoming overwrought and simply wanting to make trouble for the capitalists, they would turn to violence.

It was in this context that the Tokyo Printing strike was lost. A large number of young people, however, started to gather around *Ayumi*'s members. Shibata and Shiraishi thought that they must unite these young people into a single organisation.

Formation of the Society

The Tokyo Printing strike resulted in 150 unemployed workers. In the context of the economic depression of the time, it was a serious issue as to how these workers were to find employment.

Shibata and Shiraishi gathered the young people and explained:

---

24 *Gendaishi Shiryō* no.15, *Shakaishugi Undō* p. 235

Everyone who was sacked because of the Tokyo Printing strike has been trying really hard to find work under these depressed conditions. But, since they worked at Tokyo Printing for a long time, they have few friends in other companies. We have to do something. There is only one solution – working together to help each other. Unions are keen to come forward during a strike but they do not address the needs of workers' lives on a daily basis. That's why it is useless to look to Kantō Publishing Union for support. There is no other way for us than to create some kind of organisation to help as many as we can through our own power. The most important thing now is that young people, like you, take the lead and put in the effort for others.

These young people had seen the devoted and selfless acts of the group of workers with Shibata and Shiraishi at the centre during the strike. Their eyes lit up when they heard the story of the *Ayumi* group. That year, Shiobara, who lost his job during the Tokyo Printing strike, hosted the initial gathering to prepare for the formation of the Society at his home. After several meetings, the group was established and expanded soon after. The seeds for an organisation for the masses, that everyone had been hoping for, had sprouted. The core group of the Society was formed around Shibata, Shiraishi and Shibata Ichirō, who had been the core of the Tokyo Printing Strike committee, Sakamura, who had been the core organiser of the federation of 35 companies that had sent donations and support to the strike, and Fukui, Yamanashi and myself, who were representatives from the federation of workers from 35 companies.

My uncle managed a small print works in Shiba in central Tokyo. Yamanashi, who worked there, and Sakurai, who worked in the Ono Print Works in the neighbourhood, had been sharing accommodation in the area. Their home functioned as the Society's head office as well as the local Shiba branch office and my house became the Fukagawa branch office.

5
Fighting the enemy trying to obstruct our organisation

The Society's enemy

I will now explain the distribution of the printing industry of Tokyo, which was the focus of our activities. The largest print companies each occupied a specific area of Tokyo. The medium, small and micro print works were dispersed throughout the city, with the greatest concentration in three main areas – Kanda, Kyōbashi and Shiba. The smaller print works were concentrated in Kanda because there were a number of publishing companies that financed many publications there; this attracted printing workshops. Kyōbashi was the centre of government bureaucracy and office stationery; other printed products were subcontracted to the print works that gathered in the area. Shiba had a dense concentration of newspapers and financial and industrial magazine publishers who subcontracted their publishing to the print works in that locality. Most of the workers employed in these companies were not unionised and as a result their working conditions were very poor. In every factory, working hours, including overtime, were long – over thirteen hours a day, with only two 30 minute breaks, one at noon, one at five in the afternoon. There were only two days off a month – the first and third Sunday. With these harsh working conditions, the wages of a worker in any of the companies, including overtime, was barely enough to live on. For these reasons these areas were the stage for our activism.

The Society started off with about twenty-six members. We put out a leaflet in which we publicised the first meeting to workers in the print works in the Shiba, Kyōbashi and Kanda areas. Unlike union activism today, we did not present complicated arguments. Our most urgent task was to find work for those who were sacked in the Tokyo Printing strike, all the while trying to find new members.

The depression was increasingly severe. At the same time as the Tokyo Printing strike there were many other strikes that were mostly defensive, resisting attacks on working conditions, including sackings and wage cuts.

In the midst of all this, the war had advanced into the north of China. In order for the ruling class to prosecute the war, they had to completely suppress any resistance at home. The times had plunged into darkness.

In these conditions Shibata worked feverishly to establish the ground for the Society. He was fond of saying that:

> Militant unions are completely annihilated. Those unions which remain are in the grip of corrupt right wing labour bosses and have degenerated through their collusion with the government and capitalists. That is why they do not seriously fight for issues of workers' livelihoods, civil rights, or opposition to the war. It is natural that the masses give up on them. On the other hand, they commit nothing but vicious deeds. They rush off to lead a strike at any factory. When it is resolved they are so depraved – they deduct huge commissions from the strike funds. They're so depraved, like a bogus lawyer or something. This is why they lose the support of workers. But it is not just these leaders who are at fault, workers are also at fault. If all workers understood the importance of trade unions, became trade union members, participated in union activity, paid their dues regularly and supported their leaders so that the union officials can sustain their [workers'] livelihoods, all this would not have happened. It's a vicious cycle. In order to lead the unions to the right path, the workers themselves need to understand the importance of unionisation.

The Society started its activism by bringing concrete problems to workers on the shop floor. Members visited factories where they had acquaintances. They asked: 'Does your workplace have vacancies? If not, can you please introduce us to somewhere that might? There are many who are unemployed. If there is somewhere that can hire them, please let the Society know.' If there were any job openings, we sent over not only those who were sacked from Tokyo Printing, but also other workers in search of jobs. As already mentioned, because the majority of printworkers were not unionised they had no choice but to accept the capitalists' conditions and so their human rights had also been ignored.

Among the printworkers, those employed in the large printing companies and with the major newspapers were the aristocracy of the labour movement. Occasionally, someone would quit these companies and a vacancy would arise. If someone tried to fill the vacancy and become a permanent employee they would have to pay the manager or another senior person between 300 and 500 yen. As this was an impossible amount of money for the majority of workers, who scraped by on daily wages of up to 2 yen, printworkers had to move around from workshop to workshop as temporary workers. This was the kind of lifestyle everyone lived. Those with a wide network of acquaintances found work easily, but those who did not had to spend a month or more unemployed.

For those in the prime of their health and with skills, having no job was worse than death. In these conditions, the Society's job was to find work and help each other out.

After forming the Society and in the course of beginning our job of seeking work for unemployed printworkers, we suddenly encountered an unexpected but major enemy. It was the private employment agency, Let's Work, which advertised itself on billboards as the 'Red Cross for the unemployed'; in reality this meant it used unemployed printworkers as fodder. Job agencies today can only operate with permission from the Ministry of Labour, but back then such private job agencies, particularly this company, could be seen everywhere. Let's Work was an organisation that served the capitalists. It sent letters to all the printing bosses in Tokyo advising that 'We can easily provide workers who will work for low wages, whenever and however many you need. When you need temporary workers, by all means use Let's Work.' This agency received requests from the capitalists for all kinds of printworkers. The capitalists simply named the wage they would pay, then the agency would dispatch the requested number of workers.

In their pose as the Red Cross of the unemployed, the agency would advertise: 'Whenever you come here, there will be plenty of jobs. Please join Let's Work.' If a worker did come, after taking their details the interviewer would say: 'If only you had come a little earlier. We had an opening, but what a shame, we just gave it to someone else. Please wait. Next time we will let you know straight away.' Then they would take a 15 sen membership fee and send the worker home. If there actually was a job opening, they would let the worker take it, but the agency gave priority to its own members, applicants who brought them presents, and people who visited assiduously every day; for others, paying the membership fee was a loss. As there were no other employment agencies for printworkers, so all temporary printworkers throughout Tokyo probably made their way to this organisation at least once.

The methods of Let's Work not only affected temporary workers, but they also dragged down the wages of permanently employed workers. The task for us was to open up employment opportunities for the Society's members. Another important task was to expose the character of Let's Work. As activists we tried to create an anti-Let's Work sentiment among the entire print workforce and to bring not only activists but also the majority of printworkers to the realisation that they must come together to force the agency to stop using these methods.

In the Society's publication *Wakō no Tomo (Friends of Printworkers of Japanese Language Materials)* and in the monthly meetings, we undertook the task of completely exposing Let's Work. We argued that:

> Let's Work states that they are the Red Cross for the unemployed and that anyone who visits the agency can be rescued. But in reality it is saying unrealistic things to deceive us unemployed workers. Think about it: the number of print companies in Tokyo are limited and

naturally the number of job offers are also limited. Even with Let's Work the capitalists would never hire more than they need. This means that Let's Work is profiting from sending workers in every direction all over the city with their nonsense sweet talk. Not only that, they pressure workers to work instead of complaining, and that is pushing down the wages of permanent workers. We have to force Let's Work to alter their ways.

This complaint became relatively widely known. A number of leading members of the Society visited the boss of Let's Work and protested.

> Your methods cater to the mood of the capitalists and supply labour at wages they dictate. This results in the wages of the temporary workers as well as the permanent workers plummeting. We think this is a mistake. Among the workers there are many who are saying that Let's Work is an enemy or even that your existence is a crime on its own. We repeat we want you to consider this and rethink your methods.

As we consistently carried out this fight, it became more a process of emphasising the solidarity of workers. The Society members at every workplace constantly reiterated that:

> When our workplace needs temporary workers, it is important that we workers negotiate with the bosses before they contact Let's Work. We need to negotiate with them and try to introduce or find temporary workers ourselves. This is because if permanent workers find temporary workers, they will not bring new workers in at such low wages which might lead to their own wages getting reduced.

In this case the temporary workers should also not work for such low wages as to undercut the wages of other workers in the workplace. The outcome of this kind of activity was that the true nature of Let's Work gradually became known among activists and workers alike; they also began to understand the necessity of joining the Society. This kind of activity gradually strengthened the Society.

Let's Work frantically counterattacked the Society. It started with red baiting. 'The Society is an anticapitalist organisation. It is a grouping of reds.' Soon after, it became widely known that the head of the agency had misappropriated the money he had collected from workers and companies. He was also involved in an adultery scandal. All this destroyed his reputation, which resulted in him committing suicide. Although he was replaced, the agency only changed its ways when some young people took it over.

In the midst of strengthening militarism

Even while we continued our activism, militarism was increasing in strength. The invasion of North China gained momentum. As a result of the Kwantung Army becoming more powerful after the Manchurian Incident in 1931, the direction of diplomatic policy toward China was developed by four ministries – foreign affairs, army, navy and finance – whose aim was to completely dominate Manchuria and to step up aggression in order to acquire North China and its resources.

But the Chinese people did not just stand quietly by and accept Japan's aggression. The anti-Japanese movement spread like wildfire. The Chinese Communist Party, which undertook the Long March of 10,000 kilometres between 1934 and 1936 while fighting the Kwantung Army, argued to the nationalist Kuomintang and to all Chinese citizens that everyone must join in the fight against Japan or their nation would be destroyed. They proposed that the civil war be put on hold and tried to establish an anti-Japanese united front. The Kuomintang also appealed to the public in this way. The majority of students and workers responded positively to this appeal and the anti-Japanese movement spread throughout China. Shibata enlightened us about this situation. He educated us on the true nature of Japan's war of aggression, its recklessness, and that defeat was inevitable. This kind of analysis broadened the views of the activists.

We put our effort into completing the organisation of the Society, creating more branches and trying not just to be an employment agency but also to develop cultural and other activities.

At that time Shibata had no work, so while he was unemployed he concentrated on activism. But he had had not been able to pay his rent for six months, so he moved to Kinshichō, a working class area of Tokyo, and Shiraishi moved in and shared with him. From that time on, the second floor of Shibata's house became the headquarters of the Society and subsequently of the Club.

Not long after, Shiraishi married Watanabe Sei from the Society's Women's Section and they moved to a flat nearby. They did not get to enjoy being newlyweds for long, as their home soon became a hangout for young workers. Neither Shiraishi or Sei ever seemed to mind.

The 26 February 1936 incident

We greeted 1936 while running around all over the place engaged in Society activities. On a morning in February 1936 it had snowed heavily. We heard that there had been a major incident around the parliament building. As I was thinking about whether to go to work, Shibata, who worked in the same area as me, invited me to go along with him.

The two of us walked through the heavy snow. Getting closer we noticed that there was no one on the major roads and that barricades had been erected.

It was the day of the 26 February incident, which involved more than 1500 soldiers from several regiments. They had staged a rebellion and attacked the private residences of the inspector-general of education, Prime Minister Okada, the Finance and Domestic Affairs Ministers and the grand chamberlain. Soldiers occupied the police department and the Ministry of Domestic Affairs, the general staff office, the army and the *Asahi* newspaper office. They killed the Ministers of Domestic Affairs and Finance and the inspector-general of education, and inflicted severe wounds upon the grand chamberlain. It was announced that Prime Minister Okada was killed, but it emerged later that the head of his secretariat had changed places with him so the Prime Minister was saved. After the killing of senior statesmen, the soldiers in revolt gathered at the Prime Minister's residence in Nagatachō, the political district of Tokyo, and, combined with other forces, announced they would remove the ringleader responsible for 'the destruction of the Japanese state'.

The drama continued for three days. Martial law was declared and publications other than army announcements were prohibited. The Ministry of the Army initially referred to the group of soldiers as the 'mutinous troops', then as the 'occupation force', which quickly shifted to the 'rebel army'. Political and financial circles were not pleased with the *coup d'état* by the young officers, who demanded the establishment of military rule. It indicated that the army was about to take the strongest stance against the rebellious soldiers, due to the population becoming hostile towards the military. After this incident, freedom of speech, the press, and assembly were extremely restricted. The cause of this incident was debated in the media but the public's freedom to meet was extremely restricted. The Ministry of Domestic Affairs also banned May Day celebrations on the grounds that they would disturb public peace. From this time on until Japan lost the war and the population was liberated, we could not have May Day gatherings that had previously been held every year. Using martial law and this bloody incident as the pretext, and having defeated the coup, the military strengthened its right to express its own interests.

The strike at Yasuhisa company

The oppressive atmosphere of the time hung in the air.

Nevertheless, the Society continued to organise small gatherings and hold regular meetings in all branches. We organised a picnic to replace the banned May Day celebrations, although we could not advertise it widely to members. Eighty people – members and their families – attended the picnic held in the woods near Kinuta village, now an outer suburb of Tokyo. Looking at the attendees Shibata muttered, 'Even if circumstances get really bleak, activism can take any form'.

But the Society did not just engage in ideological debates with Let's Work. In fact, we fought two strikes at this time.

The first was support for a strike in the Yasuhisa company in Shinbashi, which employed about 30 people. The boss had decided to sack a number of workers in the name of reorganising the business. Since some employees were members of the Society, we opposed the sackings and so the owner faked the closure of the business. We established a strike headquarters in a nearby restaurant. As the struggle intensified the company brought in the Black Dragon society, a right wing organisation whose goal was the extermination of communism, so the strike became a battle between our Society and the Black Dragon Society. In labour disputes of the time, the usual method of right wing union leaders was to negotiate with the boss and do a deal to resolve the strike. But with this struggle, led by the Society, we took the issue to many factories, especially those in the local area, and gradually widened the dispute making it a concern for a greater number of workers. From Kyōbashi to Shiba our members tirelessly put up posters, handed out leaflets to workers in the local area and asked for donations. In response to all this, we received donations from various factories, and even a letter of support written by a child.

As news of the strike spread throughout the local area the strike headquarters started receiving a lot of support. In order to make it a success the Society appealed to the Tokyo Printing Union and the Council-affiliated Kantō Publishing Workers Union to cooperate and fight together to bring about the success of the strike. As a part of this joint effort we decided to hold a large joint strike conference. When we went to the police to advise them of the event, they denied permission, saying that events focusing on the Yasuhisa strike were not allowed. So the gathering took a different form, posing as a meeting featuring a speech by Katō Kanjū, a politician of the Social Democratic Party of Japan. Iwata from the Society went along as a representative of the Yasuhisa strike committee and to convey his greetings. Ultimately, the factory closure could not be overturned and the strike ended in defeat. Nevertheless, this battle brought forth a number of new activists.

The second strike was at the Sugitaya Print Works, which had hired some craftsmen through Let's Work. The strike developed because the company had decreased the rate it paid typesetters by 10 sen per page. A number of workers discussed the issue and petitioned for a 10 sen increase.

The boss replied: 'How dare you lot expect me to increase the rate for all of you. I will not increase the rate. If you do not like it, you can quit'. Sakurai and Sakamura from the Society rushed over to provide support and the factory immediately went on strike for two or three days. The surprised boss urgently notified the police, so when everyone gathered at Yotsuya station to go to work, they were followed by detectives. The company eventually brought in scabs. A fight broke out in the factory and two workers were arrested.

Sakurai, mentally prepared to be imprisoned himself, went around to have the people in custody released. But he was chased out and scolded.

> You say your wages are too low and you want the rate increased, huh. But the wages of you bastards really are not that low, are they? The daily wages of postal workers do not even reach one yen. It is just that you bastards are extravagant and asking for more than your due.

But the strike was victorious; even though it was small it ended with an increased rate.

From the Society to the Club

While Shibata was developing the Society into a mass organisation he also seems to have been thinking of a more solid structure. For this reason he put effort into developing the theoretical level of the leadership. They were mostly young people who did not know anything, since they had only a primary school education. To raise the theoretical level, we received help from a brilliant supporter.

A young man studying at the elite and prestigious Tokyo University became our tutor. He had been active in the student movement at his local high school, but he was no longer active as the student movement had deteriorated significantly. The student became acquainted with some workers and through them sought to bring meaning to his life. Coincidentally, through an introduction from his cousin, he got to know

Shibata, which is how he came to help us with our study.

A year had passed since the formation of the Society. Although we had exposed its true character, anti-communist attacks from Let's Work continued with even more intensity; they declared 'The Society is red'. We were not surprised by this slur.

The problem was that our group had stopped growing. The number of activities had increased two and a half times during the year, but we had reached a stable membership of eighty members. The reason was that, as indicated by the name, our membership was restricted to typesetters and type pickers in the Japanese language print industry, thereby excluding those printing Western books. This was because we had started out as an organisation supporting the sacked Tokyo Printing company workers during their strike. To develop we had to include all workers in the publishing and print industries, including those typesetting Western books, and in lithography and book binding as well as in publishing. Aside from exposing Let's Work, our main role had been to find work for unemployed printworkers so we had become an organisation limited to conscious activists and unemployed workers looking for work.

'We have to become the kind of organisation that workers from a wide range of workplaces will happily join, and which will develop from having a diverse membership.' This is what everyone was seriously thinking about.

It was for these reasons that the Society converted to the Club. At the time we did not know the real reason behind this, but there are stories that an organiser from the seamen's union, a communist, provided our leadership with advice about the conversion.

Later on, Sekiguchi recounted that the conversion was influenced by the JCP.

> It is not clear when or how I became acquainted with Shibata. It was 1930, on the eve of war, and because of the enemy's repression, we JCP members were forced underground, working hard to rebuild. I participated in May Day and was imprisoned for 29 days. It was the first time I woke up to class consciousness.

For several years after that I worked as an organiser with Japan Publishing, which had branches in numerous print factories. Then the Manchurian Incident broke out. It was a time when the enemy's repression intensified daily. The JCP's talented leaders – Iwata Yoshimichi and Kobayashi Takiji, were taken and killed. Also, GFL had just declared it would cooperate in the war effort, voluntarily abandoning the right to strike, which was its sole weapon. It was a period when our lives were advancing into darkness. Those of us printworkers who were left behind, no matter the circumstances, believed that the JCP would never disappear and continued with the difficult struggle while looking for their guidance.

At that time I was mentored by people including Yuga and Yamazaki, who I found out later were party members, studying tactics for organising people's fronts. I was making connections with people, wanting to build solidarity among workers in the absence of unions, and through that, I got to know Shibata Ryūichirō. I would occasionally turn up at the Society's events helping the unemployed find jobs. I informed Yuga and Yamazaki about the Society, and we received some advice from them. I believe we weren't the only ones who wanted to build a new union for printworkers rising up amidst the storm of the war, something more than just an employment agency or a social club. I remember discussing with Shibata, every time I brought him the news, the proposal to change the name to [the] Club and to strengthen the leadership. I was what you would call an underground activist type and I believe there were things that Shibata and I instinctively disagreed upon. Despite this, he always listened intently to what I had to say and I remember that Yuga and I wrote an article on page one of the first issue of *Club News*. This article was voted the top article by Club members and I remember winning train tickets as a prize.

The policy underlying the conversion from the Society to the Club was determined. The point was that as a group the Society was trying hard to change the thinking of workers but actually this was far from the only thing needed in order to take the movement forward. The fact that member numbers were not increasing was also proof. Unless the movement advanced and membership increased, the low wages of workers would never improve. To overcome this vicious cycle, the Society needed to create a group that everyone could easily join and to significantly increase membership. To draw in new members we needed to shift the focus from the streets to workplaces and to include those working in European language materials, printers and offset printworkers in addition to Japanese type pickers and typesetters.

Activists began to prepare for the conversion to the Club. I remember Shibata telling me:

> In Italy workers have clubs based on region and after they have finished work they gather at the club, drink tea, listen to music and recover from the day's fatigue. While doing so they promote friendship and strengthen solidarity. I want to create this kind of thing in Japan.

6
Aiming for a connection with the greater masses

Towards the formation of the Club

The conversion of the Society to the Club began at the end of 1936. Members started discussing the new direction. We canvassed widely to find a name that suited the character of the new group. From the huge volume of suggestions, we selected the Club.

We also leased a small two storey building in Shiba for an office. We had 100 yen in funds and the annual rent was 20 yen. Downstairs was occupied by Iwata, a central figure in the Yasuhisa strike, who served as the caretaker with his partner, who had previously been active in the JCP. To make it seem like an office one of our supporters made us a blackboard; others donated *shōgi* and *igo* sets. These were the tools we used in recruiting and developing activists. We also prepared a handmade mimeograph machine from thick cardboard paper and glass, which was very useful. It became a major tool for our activism.

In January 1937, the first new year after we began the conversion process, we combined the new year gathering with the inaugural ceremony, which we held at a local restaurant. Two hundred people attended. It was not a formal type of gathering that we might have had during the Society period, but instead we provided a stage for members to perform party pieces, songs, *rakugo* [comedic storytelling] and drama. We performed plays, including a propagandistic play based on the activities of the shopping service members,[25] and *Son* by Osanai Kaoru.[26] As expected they were extremely popular. It was a fitting start, which aimed to popularise the movement.

Shibata emphasised the following to activists, including me:

> Until now we have just opposed Let's Work, but from now on that's not enough. We have to recruit and organise a wider range of people. There are unions in the larger companies so workers can improve their living standards through the power of their own organisation. But workers in the medium, small and very small workshops have no organisation to protect their livelihoods. Our main aim for the present will be to organise these workers with low class consciousness who cannot join unions and have had no experience of their collective strength. To this end, don't launch into complicated discussions, instead get to know people. You must befriend a wide range of people, and through them, try to cooperate with the permanent workers in these workshops and develop a sense of the extent of their cooperation. There is no need to deal with the 'charred stakes', I mean people who boast that they have been involved in a union or in left wing activism, and feel that they have the authority to nit-pick or sneer at our activism. If you visit the workshops, there are a lot of young workers who are interested. What is important is to find them. If you are clear about this point and develop the movement accordingly, then the Club will grow. You can be sure of that.

Shibata thoroughly despised those who were boastful of their experience of trade unionism or being a part of the intelligentsia. Instead he focused on young people in the workplace who possessed only a limited class consciousness.

Once, a guy who used to be a part of the Yokohama City Rail Union

---

[25] Goods such as uniforms and work shoes bought wholesale and sold to members at less than market value– a form of revenue but also to help workers' meagre wages stretch a little further.

[26] A significant playwright in the New Drama movement, strongly associated with the Tsukiji Small Theatre.

leadership, but was not active at the time, came to visit and criticised the Club's activism as lame. Shibata responded by criticising him mercilessly:

> What kind of activism are you doing right now? Nothing would come out from just spitting theory without doing anything. A person's worth is not decided only on the basis of how intelligent they are. Look at those young people they're working so hard going around selling *zōri* as part of the Club's activism. They deserve to be lauded, much more than you do. Get up and act for the workers like they're doing. Sort out your theory later.

Afterwards he said:

> That guy said that when the revolution came he would be on the barricades with a gun, fighting. But anyone would be able to do that kind of thing. The important thing is how to change the present. The solidarity actions, employment mediation and shopping service type activities, whatever small and routine thing we do, we are assisting workers, gathering members and developing them and raising their class consciousness. These are the most important things. No matter how much revolutionary language you spit out, it is as useless as shit.

In this way he really encouraged us in our activism.

For the Club, the main focus was the workplace. In workplaces there were an infinite number of young workers who were a little like blank sheets of paper in terms of class consciousness. Those young people's academic record would be only six years of primary school plus two extra years of higher primary school at best and they hardly had any class consciousness or I might even say were completely ignorant of class issues. Those young workers were born into poor families, had experienced poverty throughout their lives and when they left primary school they were forced to work in order to reduce the number of mouths their family had to feed and to supplement the family income. In the workshops, their wages were low, their working hours were long and no matter how much time passed they would never get ahead. They were young people who had nothing else in life, and nothing to see ahead but a bleak, grey world. But these young people possessed the beautiful characteristics and qualities that all people in their youth have: they had a sense of justice, a mindset meant for progress, a heart longing for noble things, and the idealism of wanting a better future. And within each one of them there was a wonderful energy that enabled them to bear any hardship for justice.

The Club welcomed these wonderful resources into a single organisation, helped them to experience the joy of comradeship, and disciplined and trained them in the crucible of the Club's activism to help raise the movement up. On top of that we were developing people who would eventually be valuable in the field of class war.

Creating an organisation based on the masses

At this point I need to clarify one thing. Shibata had been a member of the much more militant NCTU, but after its total destruction, he did not join or become active in any other trade union. Instead, he chose to organise the Society, and then the Club, which took the form of social gatherings, and continued such activism until his death in prison. What was the reason behind all this?

If you consider the conditions of the time this becomes clear. It was a time when the ruling class overwhelmingly strengthened its repression of the JCP and the NCTU, both of which opposed the war. Repression of the JCP was relentless and ongoing. It was at this time that Kobayashi Takiji and Kōmiya Eitarō were arrested and murdered. On the other hand, the senior leadership of the JCP, Sano Manabu and Nabeyama Sadachika among others, recanted their communist beliefs. There were also instances of police spies in the party. All of this was a plot by the ruling class, its intention being the diminution of the authority of the JCP, which had been fighting bravely to oppose the war of aggression.

The NCTU was also suppressed several times. In February and November 1933, as well as in June and July 1934, many activists were arrested and the union almost completely destroyed.

At that time the landscape of the union movement was as follows. The current nationalist unions believed in the emperor system and held up the founding spirit of the country. But what they did in actuality was to force the mindset of labour–capital collaboration onto workers.

The labourist unions were led by right wing social democrats, but there were also left wing social democratic unions. An example of the former was GFL and of the latter the Council. At this time GFL was under the influence of the Social Masses Party, an anti-capitalist, anti-fascist and anti-communist party. In reality its three 'antis' platform forced anti-communism and labour–capital collaboration onto workers.

Needless to say, Shibata opposed these trends in the unions and I think it was natural that he refused to join them. Despite the Council steadfastly maintaining a class position and intending to form a united front, at its core were mainly public sector transport workers, with few private sector workers, so the union gained no real strength. On top of that, once the NCTU was destroyed the Special Police concentrated their attacks on the Council.

Shibata valued the high level of class consciousness in the NCTU and, for a time before the war, he was active in the union but was also strongly critical of some of its activities, which seemed superficial or just for show. He thought that as long as it did not develop an organisation with the masses as its base it would not be able to succeed in the fight to protect workers' livelihoods and rights, nor in the fight for peace in opposition to the impending war. Later, in the summer of 1930, the NCTU's policies and actions were criticised at the Profintern's 5th Congress. I think these criticisms underlay the reason that Shibata choose to base his activism around social activities. In the course of collating this book, I asked a lot of people for their thoughts on Shibata. On hearing stories from Nakajima, a post-war JCP Tokyo central district committee member who had been active in the NCTU a little before Shibata, I understood that Shibata worked hard in his activism to not repeat what he saw as the mistakes made by the NCTU. According to Nakajima:

> The NCTU was a revolutionary organisation in its thinking, but its activism of the time was full of errors. It did not think much about

the objective conditions. And so they conducted a serious self-examination upon reading the decisions of the Profintern's 5th Congress. I looked at the activism of the Club based on that self-examination. I thought that it was brilliant activism since it was carried out based on developing the various demands of workers in workplaces.

During this time, Nakajima was placed on probation and therefore did not really get involved in the Club, but he was someone who observed the Club's activities from an objective standpoint.

The developing fascist conditions meant it was becoming more difficult for trade unions just to exist legally, whether left wing or right wing. My guess is that under such conditions Shibata thought that a social activity format would be the best for organising workers. Later, some Club members repeatedly called the direction of the Club's activism mistaken, and argued that it should become a union. There were even occasions when it looked as if the organisation might split when a number of critics left the organisation. But from the beginning until the end, Shibata emphasised that it was correct to fight as an organisation based on social activity. I am sure that as the Club developed, Shibata became more and more confident that this was the right path.

The Club's activities were concrete. Within the framework of increasing membership, we gathered the names of positive young people in the factories and workshops and developed plans to conduct concrete approaches. We gathered many young, active workers around us and began to develop more facets to our activism.

The Club and the diversity of its activism

If you look at the Ministry of Industry and Commerce statistics, there were 3932 print factories and workshops in 1938, but the number of factories with more than 100 employees did not exceed 1.7 per cent. Their output was 60 per cent, while the remaining 3861 smaller factories shared the remaining 40 per cent. Working conditions were horrible, even in the large factories.

At Toppan Printing, for example, permanent staff were paid monthly, junior employees were paid either monthly or daily, and workers in the factories were paid daily. This difference in employment status also carried over into other areas of workshop life, such as use of the dormitory or staff canteen.

The usual working day was ten hours, from 7 a.m. until 5 p.m. but you had to be in the workplace ten minutes before your start time. If you were late, you were not permitted to work and would be recorded as absent. In actuality, the days were longer as there was always overtime. Company holidays, when the factory closed completely, were 1 to 4 January as well as Sundays, 30 December and New Year's Eve. These days were all unpaid.

An example of the pressure placed on workers can be seen in the calculation of severance pay. Workers could be sacked when judged by the company to have 'severely corrupted the company's morals', for having extremely 'bad character', or 'having alarming attitudes to work, despite receiving multiple warnings'. Sometimes workers could be sacked without being paid any severance pay.

Such was the situation in large companies, but they were still comparatively good. In smaller workshops the conditions were incredibly harsh. In many workshops only the first and third Sundays were rest days, overtime was an everyday occurrence and, after all this, a worker would earn only just enough to eat. For workers employed in these smaller workshops, whether they liked it or not, the conditions were ripe for them to want a group or union to protect their rights.

The Club held a meeting every month without fail. Occasionally, the Special Police would be present but when they were not there and after the main business had concluded, we discussed the domestic and international situation in a way that everyone could understand. The Club's activities gradually diversified. The shopping service, which had existed since the Society days, continued and developed further. The employment section developed stronger connections with various workplaces and actively sought out jobs for unemployed printworkers. For the unemployed who found a job but could not even afford their fare to work, the Club decided to advance them a loan of 3 yen, which would buy a month's worth of tickets on the city run train; this loan was to be paid back when they started working. This helped the unemployed overcome the hurdle of not being able to work because they could not afford fares.

The Club also developed its entertainment aspects, including a *haiku* group and frequent *shōgi* contests between teams from each workplace. When Hisaita Eijirō's 1939 play, *The Holy Family*, was performed at the Tsukiji Small Theatre, the Club rented the entire theatre for a day to hold a member-exclusive showing. The protagonist of the play is a typographer which made it easier for us to ask everyone to come along.

Through the kindness of the manager of Ono Printworks, members worked together to print the Society's newsletter. With the formation of the Club however, such an amateurish look would not suffice. The *Club News* was printed at the Tsukada Printworks in Kanda; a member who worked there had persuaded the manager to print it at a discount. We printed about a 1000 copies, which cost us 9 yen. When one of the members told the owner of the printworks about the aim of the Club and asked him to print the newsletter at a cheaper rate, the owner said, in a compassionate manner before giving us a discount:

> I think there definitely is a need for an organisation like the Club where workers can meet to develop friendships. I have always thought about the day when things would get better for workers. In the future, workers should be able to live in a comfortable environment, not in the middle of the city but in a nice house in the suburbs surrounded by flower beds. This is my only dream.

The Club greatly appreciated the owner's kindness. Our monthly membership fee was 15 sen for workers who were paid more than 1 yen per day, while others paid 10 sen. It was decided that the unemployed would pay nothing. Thus our funds were quite limited and to squeeze printing fees out of that limited budget was a tough task.

Every new year each branch held a party. While it was common for many organisations to hold parties for their members, the Club was unique in that it always found new members who would take on the responsibility of organising the entire event, from planning, to venue hire, to contacting the various workshops and the ordering of the day's proceedings. The utmost efforts of the young leadership paid off as workers from a huge number of workshops would come. The young leadership would, although in a visibly nervous and awkward manner, act as their hosts. In such a friendly atmosphere, the new year events were always a huge success.

After the party was over Shibata would always listen to a report from the new activists. Then he would exchange opinions regarding things that worked and things that could have been done better. He also offered words of encouragement and urged them on.

> You must not think that what you are doing is trivial. Through all this you are developing solidarity for and among the non-unionised workers. If we continue these activities, we can definitely foster solidarity throughout the whole of Tokyo's printworkers. It is only you young people with a sense of justice who can give themselves to working for others without thinking of your own benefit. That is what I expect you to do. Think about it — if you compare your life today to how you lived before, isn't working to help others much more worth your while?

We did not just have new year parties. Those who came along and participated in *haiku*, *shōgi* and sports carnivals initially came because these were hobbies, but at a certain stage we made them consciously organise something to develop them as activists.

New members who carried out the organising role for parties and other activities happily participated in carrying out the next activity. They carried out the activities without pay in the breaks or time they could steal from their jobs. Nakajima spoke about his impressions.

> I think Shibata placed emphasis on awakening self-consciousness in as many workers as possible so that they could constitute the working class as a revolutionary class. Nowadays there are the opportunities

to awaken such consciousness for example through elections. In the activism of those days however, there was no other way than to develop and raise the self-consciousness of workers, one by one. In this case, nothing would eventuate from gathering together armchair Marxists playing at being the intelligentsia. He considered the workers themselves as material power of workers to be important, and he believed without doubt that among them existed the conditions for creating revolutionary power. He probably saw no need for big words. The important thing was to have three or four more women workers who are inspired by Madame Curie's biography. When he talked to workers, he very carefully chose his words. He did not use the language that progressive people of the time favoured. Instead he always spoke in plain language.

Also, the Club did not just have gritty or tough people as activists. People who were mild mannered and shy and naive, with very little class consciousness were also inspired by Shibata. They thought that while what we were doing was scary it definitely was the path they needed to follow. I felt that Shibata had extraordinary capacity for guidance. I think that a mere agitator can never nurture potential activists like he did. I would say that what attracted people from the toughest to the shyest was Shibata's personality, which was so unselfish that he would give his all to the movement – in other words his charm as a revolutionary.

A union or a social group?

While we were energetically conducting our activities, an event occurred overseas which had a decisive impact on Japan. This was the Comintern's 7th Congress in 1935. At this meeting it was proposed that in order to overthrow fascism all workers in the world were to join hands and fight in the formation of an anti-fascist united front.

At this time point, fascism was gaining strength in Japan as it had after the 26 February incident. The Comintern's policy was reflected in the newspapers and magazines that began to eagerly forecast that, in order to oppose fascism in Japan, all people from the left to liberals were to gather and develop a movement for a popular front. But in Japan the JCP, which should have been the core of an anti-fascist united front, had been annihilated through repression. It was true that we saw some anti-fascist moves that were parallel to the expectations expressed in these articles.

Then the Worker, Farmer, Proletarian Council, later the Japan Proletarian Party (JPP), along with the Council and others, made a proposal to the Social Masses Party, requesting that they open the door to fight together in opposition to fascism.

Related to this an internal problem arose in the Club.

At this time Takatsu Masao, a post-war Japan Socialist Party (JSP) parliamentarian, proposed that the Tokyo Printers Union merge with the Council's Tokyo Publishing Union to form an All Tokyo Printworkers Defence League. He asked the organisations to come together to have a discussion. The Club was also invited to participate. This opportunity sparked a conflict between the main office and the Kanda branch.

The Kanda branch members differed from those in the Shiba and Fukagawa branches, in that there were several members who had previous experience in the union and student movements. For these people, the Club's direction – calling itself a social group while helping the unemployed, selling goods cheaply in workplaces and recruiting new members through baseball and *haiku* groups – was too tame. They considered it did not fit with the period. Since they had had their ideas from an earlier time, they quite naturally started to emphasise that the Club should become a trade union. Once they started thinking like this, it was only to be expected that they would not conduct the Club's activism as energetically as previously. They always put logic before action.

Shibata did not invite these people to study group sessions and did not really tell them about what he was thinking. This group probably felt that Shibata was taking advantage of the many young people who respected him, dragging them into a low level movement. The Kanda branch members' convictions were strengthened, especially in 1936, when the Social Masses Party suddenly grew from five to seventeen parliamentarians and the union movement was temporarily boosted. In this way a debate between the main office and the Kanda branch developed. Shibata and Shiraishi visited the Kanda branch every night and discussed the issue of which position to pursue.

In the end, several people left the Club and formed the Print Technicians Council with Takatsu Masao at the centre. A member who left the Club and joined the new group (and later became its Secretary) remembers:

> In the end we compromised with Shiraishi on the following point: at the time of a strike a social group like the Club would not be capable of coming to the fore and leading it. At those times the Club must bring it to the Council, and in turn we would get workers whose class consciousness is too limited that they could not join trade unions to affiliate with the Club. Shiraishi agreed with a smile. He represented the Club to offer us greetings at the inaugural meeting of the Print Technicians Council.

But, in reality the two parties never cooperated.

Shibata took a different attitude to that of Shiraishi. He unrelentingly fought against the split and even used it to educate us younger members. He explained that militant unions were being repressed one after another, so that even if we flew the flag as a union in this situation, we would end up being destroyed. Furthermore, he argued that the well-known Takatsu was actually authoritarian and that his policy would effectively take these members out of the movement. He emphasised that it was a mistake to transition to a trade union under the current circumstances. He said that the only way to support and develop an organisation in the face of violent repression was to operate like the Club, where each member could conduct activity by themselves, taking root in the workplaces to develop and nurture young people. The Kanda branch split ended with only a small number of people leaving. Three years later the Print Technicians Council no longer existed.

Shibata always took a cautious attitude on deciding how to develop the movement.

When thugs carry out blackmail, they carefully consider whether the opponent is strong or not. If the opponent is strong then they will not blackmail this person. In the same way, when thieves decide their targets they investigate thoroughly the house to break into so that they will not get caught. No thief is fool enough to enter a house the police are staking out. Needless to say in the case of our movement, it is natural to consider the power relations with our opponents.
You do not do it after you have joined the movement. Developing countermeasures against our opponents not after but before embarking upon our activism is never a cowardly thing to do. On the contrary, it's to be done as a matter of course.

Shibata used this example to explain to us the importance of carrying out activism while always keeping power relations in mind.

The proletarian parties had a significant boost in the House of Representatives election on 30 April 1937. The Social Masses Party had thirty-seven members elected, while the JPP had one member. A total of thirty-eight members were elected. In particular, the JPP's Katō Kanjū [Tokyo] received 54,000 votes, which for the time, was ground-breaking.

This meant that in the face of the JCP and the NCTU being thoroughly repressed and driven to operating underground, many workers and citizens who were antiwar, expressed their anti-fascism in voting for the Social Masses Party and the proletarian parties.

7
The unions heading to defeat through cooperation with the war

The military rode roughshod over the ambitions of working people. After the Marco Polo Bridge incident on 7 July 1937, the military strengthened its aggression towards China even further. And through all this, the labour movement leaned to the right even more.

The Social Masses Party, whose position as a proletarian party should have been that of opposition to the future war of aggression, trampled over the antiwar desires of the several million people who voted for them.

> The China Incident is a holy war for the Japanese people, through which we will contribute to the development of the civilisation of mankind by building the Far East Peace Framework with Japan, Manchuria, and China at its axis, all through exterminating colonialism and communism in China.[27]

This was how it explained the policy it had hammered out, positively supporting the war of aggression.

Even the GFL, which was under the influence of the Social Masses Party, at its October general meeting put out slogans such as 'Cooperate with industry', 'Break through the national crisis', 'Labour is a public duty' and

---

27 1937 *Shadaitō Senjika Undō Hōshin* (*1937 Social Masses Party Direction of the Movement During the War*).

'National unity'. It approved a resolution to thank the Imperial Forces and recommended complete cooperation with the war. Secretary-general of the GFL, Nishio Suehiro, even proposed a ban on strikes, which was agreed to.

It was inevitable that right wing social democrats, who support the structure of capitalism, would finally arrive at these kinds of statements.

The ruling classes, beginning with the military, encouraged by the right wing social democrats' stance of cooperation with the war, not only strengthened the war of aggression even further, but on 15 December 1937, arrested over 4000 people who mostly belonged to the JPP and the Council. Then, on 22 December, both organisations were banned.

The reason given for the ban was that 'The Japan Proletarian Party intends to change the national polity and its policy of establishing an anti-fascist people's front is that of the Comintern'.[28]

Thus within the union movement, all influential sections that had fought to oppose the war from a class standpoint were erased. The population had no choice but to be mobilised to fight the war of aggression. Such trends cast a dark and stifling pall over those of us who were active in the Club. The wartime mood rapidly strengthened and increasing numbers of young people were conscripted. Everywhere throughout the town soldiers were leaving for the front while people seeing them off sang 'We shall win'. Their families desperately wanted their loved ones to come home safely; as if clutching at straws, they would request passers-by to contribute a stitch to the thousand stitch campaign.[29]

Popular military songs, such as the *Bivouac Song* and *Off to Fight the Bandits*, had sad melodies perhaps to appeal to the public about the hardship of soldiers at the front.

The war violence was ramped up and military expenditure expanded. In 1937–38 it was the enormous figure of 73.8 billion yen.[30] The government did everything it could to squeeze the money out of the population. Taxes

---

28 *Kindai Nihon Rōdōsha Undō Shi (The History of Japan's Modern Union Movement)*: 170.

29 Sewn on to a piece of cloth as an amulet and sent to soldiers at the front to keep them safe.

30 Equivalent to approximately $A460 billion in today's money.

were increased and the national debt was published. The population was encouraged to save and inflation was accelerated. If not for these things they would not have been able to secure this enormous military budget. They continued to strengthen the exploitation of the people, beginning with the working class.

Pouring effort into training activists

Wars mobilise everyone and everything for their sake. In March 1938 the National Mobilisation Law was introduced. The aim was not only to mobilise peoples' lives and livelihoods for the war effort but also to completely ban strikes, debate, publications and meetings. Electricity was put under state control, the manufacture of all products, including cotton, was regulated.

As a result of these policies, even in our printing industry, it became extremely difficult to get hold of the chemicals and products necessary to make printing ink. Since such materials were designated as military materials, the printing industry suffered severely.

The problem was not just a lack of materials. An oppressive atmosphere was encroaching upon our activism, as if to suffocate us.

In order to pursue the war, the Special Police became very vigilant; they searched out antiwar elements and increasingly repressed them.

Here are some examples of articles detailing the typical repression of people that the mainstream newspapers of the time were enlivened by. In February 1938, thirty-eight members of the Worker–Farmer Faction were arrested, in September fifty-four members of the underground JCP were arrested, in October publications by the University of Tokyo's Professor Kawai were banned, in November twenty-nine communists involved in the Materialism Study Group were arrested and in December thirty-seven people from the left wing group that had formed in the dormitory inside the Tōyō Rayon factory in Shiga were also arrested. Prosecutions in this year also included 104 associated with the JCP, 103 associated with the JPP and twenty-eight from the Young People's Federation for New Religion.[31]

---

31 Tamiya 1948: 163.

As for the union movement, it continued its complete turn to the right. The Tokyo Printworkers Union finally disbanded. Then, the PIA, the purpose of which was to serve the war effort, was initiated and promoted by the right wing leadership of the Tokyo Transport Workers Union and the Seafarers Union.

Even in these violent conditions, the Club continued with little fanfare to put all its effort into enlarging its membership and nurturing activists.

Shibata held the following firm conviction:

> Whatever the period is like, there are without doubt activists in the workplace who have leadership qualities. The worse workers' lives become, more and more of these activists will stand up to take correct action. The most important thing to do now is to find these activists, have them participate in Club activism and give them training.

We looked for activists everywhere and the Kanda branch of the Club was rebuilt with new activists at the core. Taguchi spoke about that time:

> I participated in the Club in 1937, when I was working at the Kondo Print workshop in Shiba. I heard about the Club from Sugiura Masao. I was also angry and dissatisfied that no matter how hard workers worked, our lives continued to be harsh. Sugiura told me about the reason for all this and of the real enemy. He suggested I read *The Second Story of Poverty* by Japanese Marxist Kawakami Hajime and Marx's *Wage Labour and Capital*. Soon I joined the Club and Sugiura introduced me to Shibata. He talked passionately about how as long as workers do not fight collectively, they will never be liberated.
>
> The strongest, lasting memory I have of that time is when I participated in the Club's activism with Sugiura and others. I was active in the Kyōbashi area. In order to recruit non-unionised workers for the Club, I went around factories selling *zōri*. There were many hard times, including snowy nights, but I was flooded with the conviction that this activity was extremely important. The basis of

my conviction was what Shibata had told me. Shibata gathered all
the activists of the time at his house, and enthusiastically explained
how and by whom the workers were exploited and that the only way
to free workers from exploitation was to build solidarity, thereby
transforming capitalist society into a socialist society. He then told us
that we ourselves held the responsibility to pursue this work. Thanks
to Shibata enlightening us ideologically, we were able to carry out our
activities every day and every night with great joy. Such guidance
made it possible for us young people to live with such big dreams
despite the social conditions of the time.

Whenever we didn't know what to do or there was a point we
didn't understand in the books we were recommended, we would
go to Shibata's house to ask. We always visited him about 11pm or
sometimes as late as after 12 midnight. As it was so late, the door was
locked, but when we called out he would quickly come downstairs and
with all smiles would invite us in and listen to what we had to ask. He
would then give us the appropriate advice. The thing that impressed
me the most, even now, was that it didn't matter how late it was he
would always be reading. At first I even wondered when he slept.

And no matter how late we visited, we could talk to him about
everything and he would provide good advice.

On those occasions Shibata's extremely short-sighted eyes would
gleam making him look like the embodiment of enthusiasm. During
those days, visits to Shibata gave me great courage and I would
go home feeling more confident. Since just meeting him gave me
confidence, even when I didn't have any particular reason to visit, I
would still go and see him.

Also he often got me to write for the Club newsletter. No matter what
he made me write, whether it was an article about the sports carnival
or the *shōgi* competition, it would always be a story emphasising the

necessity of worker solidarity. Looking back they were extremely simple articles but at the time it took a lot of effort. He always praised me and then drew out points from my article which reflected class consciousness, developed my understanding by emphasising the significance of these viewpoints and urged me on.

Then he would recommend another book to read. He would of course recommend theoretical books but what was especially characteristic of him was that he recommended a lot of novels. Recalling it now I cannot emphasise enough that what made him a great mentor was that he always tried to educate us not only by making us read formal books but also through protagonists in novels. I read a great deal of Russian literature learning a lot and gaining much courage from them.

Leaders in a difficult period

As you can see from the impressions of key Club activists, Shibata was an excellent person. What comes to my mind when I think of Shibata is him sitting at his humble desk, in the perfect pose of resting on his haunches, intently reading under a dim electric light. When I asked many activists of the time for their memories of Shibata, they all answered in the same way.

As he sat in front of his desk, in that dark period when fascism was on the rampage, he was guiding the Club, which, at its highest point, had 1500 members. It goes without saying that when serious issues in the Club occurred, Shibata would leave his desk to direct the situation.

During the time of the Society, Shibata rotated every night between the houses of several members that served as hangouts, and worked at the forefront to build an organisation. If I remember correctly, he stopped coming to the front of activities and, after the Society converted to the Club, sat at his desk instead. I remember once asking the reason.

> The Club has to be a mass organisation which lots of people can join. For it to develop, theory is more and more necessary. Someone

has to study. From now on, I will take that role. I will not be able to come along to the main office and branch meetings as often as before. Instead of me, Shiraishi and all of you have to become the core of the movement.

At first, this might sound like a selfish reason. But he placed a hard responsibility on himself, so much so that it was beyond reproach. He never left the typesetting workplace throughout his whole life. He would go to his workshop every morning with a lunchbox in hand, work overtime, have dinner when he got home, and spend little or no time with his family before going up to his room to read.

There is another possible reason why he stopped coming out to the front. The Club was developing itself as a thoroughly legal organisation under the scrutiny of the PPL. In that situation, with Shibata's history of arrest as an NCTU member, if he had been prominent it would have drawn the attention of the Special Police. I guess that he thought it was safer and more appropriate for nurturing activists to manage the Club through Shiraishi and not come to the forefront himself.

But can a mass movement be guided from behind a desk? Surely anyone would have doubts about this. I wouldn't be able to accomplish something like that even if someone were to tell me to do so today. The reasons Shibata accomplished it are first, that he had thoroughly absorbed scientific socialism. Even when young people brought him the most difficult questions, he could give them the right guidance from a class perspective. Second, he was very good at leadership and developing people. Third, he had an excellent personality. He was an appealing mentor for young people and he was widely admired by them. Incidentally, he always had one or two key activists staying at his house with him. For a time it was Shiraishi. But when he married and moved to nearby Shibata, Taguchi and Kōmiya moved in with Shibata. In this way, more than anyone else, Shibata was able to keep abreast of what was happening in the Club overall – about the entire Club through Shiraishi, about the Fukagawa and Kyōbashi branch through Taguchi and about the Kanda branch from Kōmiya. His house was also where the Club library and the purchased goods for distribution were kept. Thus activists representing the respective areas were always coming to his place to exchange books or pick up goods. These young people also came to ask his advice. It did not matter how late it was, when we went up to his room from the back door, he would be sitting at his desk intently reading. When he saw us he would smile and say, 'Job well done' showing his appreciation for our efforts. Then we would give a report and ask him about problems we had come up against. Immediately, he would offer some appropriate points. In this way, every time it became clear what we had to do next, we felt as if our eyes were opened for the first time and gained more confidence.

As Taguchi has already said, at the end of every visit he would always recommend we read. The books he recommended were books that awakened a sense of justice within us, or books that filled us with courage. For those with a more advanced consciousness he would recommend books that would open your eyes to class issues. Watching how Shibata guided us members, I learnt that guidance was not only about fighting out front but it was also important to grab the nucleus, to encourage people in their activism and to do all this systematically.

8
Keeping a low profile working among the masses

Working to double the Club's membership

In 1938, in the midst of war, the new year party was held at Sakamura's house. A policy to expand the Club by doubling the number of members from the current 700 was adopted. However, conflict arose between the old and new leadership. In looking back to that time Kōmiya recalled that

> Shibata's uniqueness was that he never made decisions alone. Before embarking on the move to double the organisation he made certain preparations. Even though the Club had parted ways with the Takatsu faction, among those who had been members from the Society period there were some who thought that with the Club becoming a more mass-based organisation it would amount to losing its class consciousness. They also doubted the significance of gathering new members for the purpose of strengthening the Club when these new faces were unable to tell the difference between the Club and Let's Work. These people brought up this debate everywhere, which tended to confuse the new activists.
>
> Sakamura's house was deliberately chosen as the venue for the new year party. Here, young activists mixed with the more experienced members. They could hear discussions about principles in the

development of a mass organisation and relevant issues. This developed into a clear criticism of the Takatsu faction, helped them understand the rationale for the move to double the membership of the organisation and gave them confidence in developing it. When Shibata came to one turning point, he would employ such methods providing activists with theory and practice combined.

The decision to double the size of the organisation was developed in the following way. We printed a survey sheet listing hobbies that workers in the factories might have and took them around to various factories. This survey could be conducted as long as we had one Club member in each factory.

We conducted the survey in our own factories and compiled the data with the help of other Club members. This would later form a political map for organising the factory. The compiled data made it all obvious at a glance: in this factory there are this many workers who like movies, in another many who like *haiku* or mountain climbing or reading. There was nothing else but the cultural demands the workers had. It was crucial for us to help fulfil these demands.

Having gained insights from the survey results, activists organised contacts between workers using the data. For instance movie lovers would take on responsibility for organising a film appreciation group and invite people who also loved films in other factories along to screenings. Afterwards, over tea and snacks, the person responsible would open up discussion about the film. After discussing what people enjoyed or thought was good or not very good, they would arrange another screening. Through the multiple screenings they would develop a friendship and the new faces would be encouraged to read the Club newsletter. The crucial thing here was to make sure those in charge of the screenings became new activists.

The same would happen for other activities, such as hiking in the mountains and *haiku*. Historically, there had been a lot of *haiku* lovers among printworkers so we asked several well-known *haiku* poets, who were printworkers themselves, to select a seasonal topic for the *haiku* that would be circulated among the factories. The submitted poems would be published in our *haiku* journal, which was again circulated to factories in order to collect votes for the best one. The results of the vote would be published in the next issue of the journal and, simultaneously, submissions would again be called for. Since restricting the activity to the pages of the journal might be boring, this group also organised *haiku* gatherings that attracted large numbers of participants.

Haiku enthusiasts were generally the older and more experienced workers who, to a certain extent, had some influence in their workplaces, so gaining their support made the Club's organising activities much easier. By having a *haiku* journal appearing regularly, naturally activists needed to visit the factories two or three times a month to gather poems for the journal or to distribute the journal in which the poems were published. Such activities were done by members who themselves enjoyed *haiku*. These activists soon realised that the real aim of these activities was to organise printworkers. In addition, we gained information about the factories as well as more members for the Club. We would also purchase shoes and clothing and sell them around the factories to workers for 20–30 per cent less than [what they cost] in the local shops. Factories of the time did not have in-house shops. Therefore, when activists visited factories selling these goods they were welcomed everywhere. In this way we maintained contact with numerous factories.

The problem was always practice. It was important to connect workers in different workplaces, but the class consciousness of workers in workplaces varied. We needed to grab those workers who had a well-developed class consciousness. This role was undertaken by the reading fraction. Initially, we started with books that Shibata owned, but to create a book club we appealed to workers in all factories to donate even just one book. We received a huge number of books and compiled a list. We visited factories and lent books to those interested in reading. Activists frequently visited the factories operating a lending library. With some time to chat, they were able to gain more understanding of the readers' interests and class awareness through the books they borrowed.

In order to further develop these activities, in the autumn of 1938 we organised a big sporting event. This event revealed the results of our activities so far – 450 members attended and the day was a success. I think it was the high point of the Club's activities. A participant recalls: 'A friend and I participated. Observing the event, my friend and I discussed whether it would be alright to gather so many people. We thought we might get repressed.'

Shibata did not even make a mistake on this point; he had a well thought out plan. As camouflage, everyone sang the military patriotic song, *'Miyo! Tōkai no sora akete'* ['Ah! Behold the sky above the eastern sea'].

While developing our activities in this way, with the workplace as the foundation, we also put out a call to workers for a slogan so that the Club's name would become familiar to everyone. Of those suggested, the slogan 'Good people, Good skills,[32] Good Club' was selected as most representative of the Club's character. All of the activists had confidence in this slogan because it appealed to any print workplace and in the midst of harsh repression it could confound the Special Police. Shibata also emphasised that activists must in fact have good skill. 'Even if your reasoning is really good, if your skill is poor the masses won't follow you. More than reasoning, let's improve our skill. Then everyone will respect that.'

The Club's overt activities have been described above. The leadership, however, was divided into grades and continued to develop its education. From time to time, the previously mentioned student from the University of Tokyo would come and tutor us. The books we read and studied included translations of Lenin's *What is to be done?*, *the Foundations of Leninism* and the *Analysis of Japanese Capitalism*. The Club's Women's Section read works that included Bebel's *On Women* and *The Biography of Marie Curie*.

These books were heavily redacted by the censors but the study group would fill in the blanks and made the participants read the books within strict time limits.

Japanese translations of books on scientific socialism, Marxism and Leninism were still available in book shops. Pocket editions especially were perfect for us since they were relatively inexpensive and also small

---

32 The word used here is *ude*, which literally means arm but which can also be translated as skill. In this instance it has a double meaning, that is, on the surface it can mean skill as printworkers but also in the context of what the Club did, it means political skill in recruiting and developing class consciousness.

enough to fit into a pocket. We were very happy that we could walk around carrying them without being obvious. Since these books were commercially available, theoretically speaking there should be no problems if someone bought these books and read them. Setting up a study group using these books as textbooks was a different issue. This was a time when the Special Police would be sure to raid the gathering, make arrests and carry out background checks while torturing the arrested and treating the whole process as authorised under the PPL. The study groups often ended very late so we had to be careful when making our way home. For this reason, we left any really thick books we were reading at Shibata's house, but we could take these pocket-sized books home to read. We hid them in the folds of our underwear so that when the cops patted us down they would not know where they were hidden. The main streets had police boxes that had a cop on duty 24 hours a day. Under the Police Peace Law they had the authority to call over anyone walking around, search them, ask them to strip and conduct a body search as well as arrest people without warrants. Even the lowest ranking cops had these rights.

When walking home it was important to avoid these police boxes. If you did meet a cop on his rounds, it was necessary to have prepared an excuse as to why you were out late. When challenged by a cop with 'Oi, where are you going?', for example, our regular excuses were that we were about to visit our aunt who was in a critical condition or that we were returning from the rite of watching over a dead relative's body. We made sure we were fluent in reciting the address of where we were heading to or had been.

But the continuation of the study group was a demanding task as all members were regularly working thirteen hour days as well as carrying out a lot of Club activity.

Most of the activists had graduated only from primary school so our knowledge base was quite low. Moreover, the books of the time were difficult, unlike books we have today, where writers who are also social science teachers break everything down to facilitate workers' understanding. For these reasons the study group did not readily advance. When Shibata met with activists the phrase he continually repeated was 'Read books, read books'. He said, 'When you get into bed, read for five or ten minutes. It is

OK if you fall asleep while reading. If you continue this, then reading will become a habit and you will soon feel like you can't help but read.' This was his stock argument.

Shibata read everything – books that would develop young people or books that raised class consciousness – before recommending them to others, and then he would tell the young people about the content of the book with great passion. On hearing Shibata talk, people would end up feeling that they must read that book.

The books I remember from among those we used for the study group include Kawakami Hajime's *The Second Story of Poverty*, Marx's *Wage Labour and Capital*, Engels' *Socialism: Utopian and Scientific*, *The Communist Manifesto*, Lenin's *Left-wing Communism: An Infantile Disorder* and *One Step Forward, Two Steps Back*, and Piatnitsky's *Organisational Questions*.

But more than theoretical texts, what really enlightened us young people was novels, including Gorky's *My University*, Petrov's *The Little Golden Calf*, Ostrovosky's *How the Steel was Tempered* and *The Storm*, Sholokhov's *And Quiet Flows the Don* and *Virgin Soil Upturned*, Kobayashi Takiji's *The Crab Cannery Ship* and Tokunaga Sunao's *The Street without Sunlight*, Sui Hajime's *Cotton* and *A Shimizuyaki Scene* and Shimaki Kensaku's *Quest for Life*. [This last was based on the author's experiences of working at a printing company, going on strike and being sacked]. The Club's Women's Section read, among others, Gorky's *Mother*, Agnes Smedley's *Daughter of the Earth*, Marie Curie's biography, Nozawa Fumiko's *The Brick Factory Girl* and Yoshino Genzaburō's *How Do You Live?*

We also read essays, such as Agnes Smedley's 'China Fights Back: An American woman with the Eighth Route Army' and 'Michelangelo' by Hani Gorō, which, while not novels, broadened our perspective nonetheless. All these books were difficult to read, but in reading Gorky's *My University*, we saw the protagonist, who was in the same pitiful circumstances as us, grow up treating society as his university, and we in turn gained confidence in our way of living. In reading Ostrovosky's *How the Steel was Tempered*, we were deeply touched with the protagonist Korchagin's revolutionary passion and promised ourselves to learn from him.

After reading the books Shibata recommended, he would ask our impressions and on hearing what impressed us he would respond, 'I see, that's good', and suggest another book. Through this process we gradually developed class consciousness. This way of guiding was adopted by all Club members. Taniguchi from the Kanda branch commented:

> Shiraishi came three times a week. Everyone would gather round and he would read to us books like Shimaki Kensaku's *Quest of Life* or Tokunaga Sunao's *The Street without Sunlight*. He'd say it's OK to stretch out on the floor and relax while you listen.

I also recommended books to others that had impressed me.

Activism at the Beach House

In the summer of 1939, we rented a house by the beach in Enoshima and for two months from July it was a part of our activism. On Sundays, many workers would come to stay and relax. The purpose was to organise non-unionised workers. We would borrow bedding from members. Shiraishi vacated his house in Tokyo and lived at the beach house as caretaker for the two months. We also used it as the venue for educating leaders. The Beach House Regulatory Committee was located at the Club headquarters and when we had booking requests from various workplaces, the committee would decide who could use the Beach House. We would try our best to facilitate the booking requests from important workplaces [for recruiting], even if that entailed turning down requests from other workplaces. When promising potential activists visited us, we would invite them down to the beach at night and discuss all sorts of things with them. On days other than Sundays and public holidays we would invite the members' children to come and stay for a week. These gatherings had extremely important outcomes and so we did it again in 1940. Shiraishi's wife Sei, who managed the Beach House, commented:

> In the summer of 1939 we moved from the house we had had since our marriage to the Enoshima Beach House. Shibata had said to me

'You have been unwell since you started having a household but if you went to Enoshima, you might feel somewhat better. Take it easy while you're there'. But there was no time to take a breather. For two months Shiraishi commuted to the Diamond Printing Company in Shiba and on Saturdays and Sundays workers would come in groups from workplaces everywhere. I was run off my feet with cooking and making tea.

Katō who was working at the Diamond Company with Shiraishi at the time commented:

The Beach House was hugely welcomed by printworkers who had no places to have fun. On Saturdays and Sundays it was packed with workers from various branches. In the middle of it all were the activists who were mobilised to cook curry rice and pork soup, so it was far from a seaside resort for them.

Nakajima a former NCTU member, said:

There was this moment when I was very impressed observing Shibata's interactions with young activists at the Club office. It was about the Beach House. If Shibata had opened his mouth, the dispute would have been settled in an instant. But instead he patiently made them state their opinions and got them to debate it. Both soon started to get a little excited and emotional. Then he gave them one or two words of advice. 'The Beach House is not just a place for fun, although it is important for printworkers' recreation.' With that they both calmed down and came to an agreed conclusion. He never failed to make everyone take time to discuss things, and then, when the dust settled, there was always a consensus.

When I stayed at the Beach House it was being used for workers' education. If I remember correctly, a journalist from Dōmei Press talked of the international situation. He explained about the geography

Gathering of *Ayumi* group 1934; (below) Picnic of *Ayumi* group at Kinuta village May 1936

Picnic of *Ayumi* group at Kinuta village May 1936; (below) Club inauguration ceremony 14 January 1937.

(Clockwise from top left) Club flag. The text says (reading from right to left) the name of the Club in Japanese: *Shuppankō Kurabu*; Masao Sugiura's first wife Tomiko Nishida. She was a printworker as well as a member of *Shuppankō Kurabu*; Two members of the Club at the Enoshima Beach House July-August 1939.

Club baseball match at Tuskishima (Tokyo) ground 1939; (below) At the Club's Enoshima Beach House probably 1939 or 1940.

(Clockwise from top) Notification of 1944 sentence of Club member Mitsuo Shiraishi; Cover of the second Japanese edition of this book, published in 1981 as *Wakamono wa arashi ni makenai: Senjika insatsu shuppan rōdōsha no teikō* (Young People Will Not Lose to the Storm: The Resistance of Print and Publishing Workers During the War); Cover of the first Japanese edition of this book, published in 1964 as *Senjichū Insatsu Rōdōsha no Tatakai no Kiroku* (Record of the Struggle of Printworkers during the War). Masao Sugiura still active in recent years.

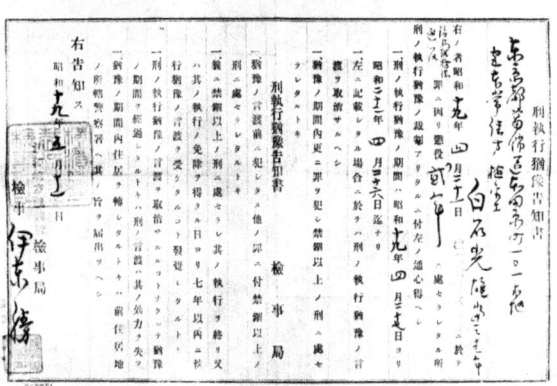

(Clockwise from top) Masao Sugiura and Kaye Broadbent 12 June 2018. Photo courtesy of Hiroto Fujita; Commemorative stone to the Club (*Shuppankō Kurabu*), erected in November 1977 in Jogan temple, Tokyo. Japanese Communist Party Chairman Nosaka Sanzō provided the calligraphy on the stone which states: 'Commemoration stone to *Shuppankō Kurabu*.'; Memorial stone to the Club (*Shuppankō Kurabu*) erected in November 1977 in Jogan temple, Tokyo. Photos courtesy of Kaye Broadbent. The inscription reads:

'In 1935 with the Zenkyō union's Shibata Ryūichirō and Shiraishi [Mitsuo] at its core, print and publishing workers established the Society. In 1937 it became the Club. In the midst of harsh wartime repression the Club had 1500 members in over 100 workshops. In 1940 most of Japan's unions were absorbed into the PIA but the Club resisted. Through covert activism it protected the livelihoods and rights of workers as well as carrying out anti war activities. In 1941 many were arrested by the Special Police and three were tortured and murdered. In February 1945, without recanting [his commitment to communism] Shibata died in prison. At the end of the war Club members formed the All Japan Printing and Publishing Workers Union and worked hard to establish democratic print works. In 1947, having achieved its purpose, the Club disbanded.

This memorial will exist forever. November 1977.'

of Spain, France, Germany and the Balkans, and the three northern European countries, as well as about the status of Japan and the United States. By this means he clarified international power relations and especially the differences between the union movements in Japan and in the various European countries. Then someone asked, 'Why is Japan like this?' The explanation naturally moved on to how the imperial system of Japan is connected to the bourgeoisie and capitalists and how it exploits the Japanese population.

At this point, Shibata asked the journalist to stop because you could not be entirely sure who was present at the Beach House, that is, there may have been informers. I saw with my own eyes that Shibata was aiming to educate the young people with patience rather than getting into agitation and thought that Shibata's activism was consciously planned and developed, far from a spontaneous social gathering.
The attention the Club paid when developing its movement was so impressive that I was moved beyond words.

The Beach House ended after two months. The Shiraishis then leased a coffee shop in Kanda that became the stronghold of the Kanda branch.

Activity centred on workshops becoming more difficult

While we were carrying out our activities, the world was becoming increasingly dark and control over workers was getting stronger and stronger. In 1939 a series of laws was introduced that forced reporting of the skills, restricted wages, extended working hours and regulated the hiring of employees. All of these restrictions were assiduously carried out with the purpose of ensuring a stable labour force. Despite all this there were still labour shortages, so the National Requisition Ordinance was introduced, which meant that workers could be pressed into working in munitions factories at any time.

In the mainstream newspapers there were many stories of organisations being repressed, including reading groups, social gatherings, the Esperanto movement, magazine circles, the movement to render Japanese language into Roman script, student organisations and consumer cooperatives. The newspaper reports treated them as though they were part of the red movement with links to the Comintern's anti-fascist popular front. Until this time repression had been aimed at the upper levels of organisations, but now it focused on the organisations of working people.

Despite this atmosphere the Club continued its activities, which focused on the cultural demands of the workplaces. We were also nurturing new activists. One such new activist gave his impressions.

> I passed the conscription exam as a rank B-2 soldier, but soon the army put me in the higher ranked B-1 group. In 1938 I was called up and taken to Shandong, China. I came home in less than six months however, since I was told that substitute personnel were unnecessary and thus my call up was cancelled. I started working at a factory but they paid me very little, so I got fed up with them and moved to a larger workplace in Kanda. Even in this factory, there were many trainees turned type pickers who urged me to work hard, but the wages were still low. So I skipped work there to look around at factories in other places but I had no luck. It was the same everywhere.
>
> I remember feeling like the reality of my life was being thrust into my face and I became quite gloomy. When I was deep in thought about this one lunch time, Sugiura tapped me on the shoulder. Although we were working in the same workplace, our levels were different, so I had never spoken to him, but I knew he was a leader in the Club. Fearlessly, Sugiura frequently challenged or opposed our arrogant foreman who always yelled at us while he sat in front of a desk in the middle of the huge typesetting area. I witnessed Sugiura's bravery from behind the cases that contained the type, and was always surprised and impressed.
>
> Slowly and haltingly I told Sugiura how I felt. I can't remember precisely what he said to me, but the conversation concluded with

him telling me to cheer up and inviting me to assist with the Club tasks. Suzuki also came over and encouraged me.

It was around the time when branches of the PIA were being formed in each company. Shima Makoto, the son of the company president, often gathered all the workers at the workshop and gave us admonishing lectures. I heard that this Shima Makoto, who used to be a student activist while in one of the imperial colleges, gave it up due to horrible torture he had to endure when he was arrested. When he talked, his face twitched due to facial neuralgia caused by the torture.

Shima Makoto advised Sugiura that he wanted to discuss with young members of the Club about his idea of forming a youth division for PIA in his company. We discussed this and decided that I, along with eight other members who all were young type pickers, were to go and have a talk with Shima Makoto. He explained his idea of forming a youth division and asked us for our opinion.

It was our first time attending anything close to a conference, and nobody had ever stated their own opinions in front of so many people. On top of that, we were facing the cherished son of the president who had experience in activism. Nobody dared to say a word. So, I mustered all my courage and said something like: 'I understand your side, but I don't feel comfortable with simply following directions given from above without any autonomy. If we must do this, please at least let us create the organisation with our own hands.' Shima Makoto sternly stared at my face for a while, and then said, 'With our own hands, huh?' as if to sneer at me. After that, he just fell silent. No more talks were held regarding the youth division, and soon, as Shima Makoto died, the idea fizzled out.

We usually spent our lunchtimes contacting members in other factories, distributing the newsletter, collecting dues or delivering the goods people had ordered. In order to use the time efficiently, we would secretly eat our lunch during working hours so that at the moment the lunch bell rang, we would race over to the company bicycle and speed off on our errands.

The quality of our lives continued to deteriorate. The government had placed goods and the workforce under state control. We workers suffered under the impact of inflation, the working hours were lengthened and a piece rate system was forced on us. On the other hand, there were labour shortages in the factories due to the number of soldiers needed on the war front. Employers made full use of the wartime conditions to introduce the temporary employment system in all industries. This was in spite of the fact that they could have hired people full-time because they were receiving money from the government.

Inflation led to an upsurge in the demand for wage increases. The government issued the Price Control Order to halt price increases and the Wage Pegging Policy to peg prices and wages to the level that existed on 18 September 1938. But prices continued to increase due to the black market and daily necessities became even more unavailable and unaffordable. As wages were held down, workers' lives became harsher.

With the continuation of the war the union movement met further repression, but the Club continued to penetrate the workshops more deeply. Membership continued to increase. Most workshops had two or three members while others had up to ten members. Below is a list of factories where we managed to gain members. Some of these were well-known companies and some still exist today. Some branches had Club members in up to 60 per cent of all factories in their area.

- Kanda branch: 28 factories, including Tetsudō Kōsaikai, Dōkōsha [publisher], and Tsukada Printing
- Shiba branch: 29 factories including Tokiwa Printing and *The Japan Times* [newspaper]
- Kyōbashi branch: 42 factories including Sanyūsha [publisher], Harada Printing and Daiichi Printing
- Others: 12 factories including Kōbunsha and Shōbunsha [publishers].

How was the Club able to develop during this repression?

For the Club the connection with the factories was extremely important. If there was someone to take the place of a member when they left their factory, we would establish them as the contact person. If there was not, we asked the member who was leaving to find a replacement. Even so, there were still cases where people quit their workplaces without notifying the Club and we lost contact with them. In these cases a member would visit that workshop and try to find a replacement. Whenever we heard rumours about potential new Club members in workshops without a contact, we would visit them regardless of whether we knew the person or not. We would ask if they would like to receive the newsletter, or would invite them to various meetings in order to try to build up that connection and gradually encouraged them to become members. Such was the method we took.

During wartime, when workers demanded pay rises or went on strike, the Special Police would rush over and swallow the boss's story without question, immediately arrest the leaders, and check their background and ideological beliefs. This was what labour–capital relations were like back then.

It is important to delve into how we expanded in these times of intense repression. Because of these conditions, it was rare to see workers raising economic demands but this did not mean that they had no demands to make. Workers did have a diverse range of demands. They wanted jobs, they wanted to be able to purchase goods cheaply because their wages were so low, and they wanted their cultural demands met. When their demands were put forward, workers were supportive and became involved. In this way, our activism was proof that when demands were sincerely taken up, movements would surely develop, even in the face of the most brutal repression.

From that perspective, let us look at how we took up workers' demands

On entering the Club's office the first thing you would see was a huge blackboard. On it was written the names of companies looking for workers. Someone would be sitting there and anyone who was looking for work would be able to consult them about the job. If the applicant did not have the train fare, they would be lent money. If the person was unemployed and had no money for food, a member would take them to the nearest cafe to eat before heading off to the workplace, putting the meal on the member's tab. As this became a financial burden for members, we eventually stopped doing this.

In the office there were many *shōji* and *igo* boards so members could play whenever they wanted. In the early period we also ran a harmonica class. We had bought a lot of harmonicas from a wholesaler, and a member taught a class.

A *haiku* magazine was published monthly and a *haiku* gathering was occasionally held in a nearby restaurant. I remember a great number of activists coming together to publish this magazine, from the printing to the binding and everything.

We even had a baseball team called Printing Labour Club, which occasionally played the teams from some of the larger printing companies. Since a member lived near the baseball ground, the Club's Women's Section, who came down to cheer the teams on, would bring the players water in buckets. Occasionally, we would attend the theatre. I still remember the plays we saw in the local theatres. The film screenings were also unforgettable. We often saw French, Russian and Japanese movies. We also took day trips to the beach and fairgrounds, and organised hiking trips.

The selling group sold items at cost price to workers, including personal items such as shirts, *zōri*, razors, visors and work tools, and household goods such as charcoal and shoji screen paper used for repairing internal doors in Japanese houses. As for financial losses they could not be recovered from selling goods, so we supplemented them by selling the boxes that contained the goods.

The book club received donations from workers in a huge number of factories to establish a lending library. New books were purchased monthly to expand the collection. Shibata's sister, also a printworker and Club member, created a list of books but excluded titles that would cause a problem if seen by the authorities. She circulated the list to the workshops, enabling workers to reserve books they wanted to read. This also helped to maintain connections between the workshops.

The Club's Women's Section developed its own list of activities, including cooking and kimono sewing classes as well as book club meetings.

The biggest event was the sports carnival, which was organised by activists in all the branches and included events such as a tug of war for which each workplace would field a team.

This is how a typical day went for me.

My mother would wake me at 5.30 am. I would hurriedly wash my face and gobble down breakfast. With my lunchbox in one hand I would dash out of the house. If I walked I would not make it, so I ran to the train stop and got to work narrowly escaping being late. I changed into my work clothes, picked up my tools and got to work. Five minutes before lunch time I would secretly eat my lunch and, in the 30 minutes we had for lunch, I would visit two or three workplaces close by and complete my tasks. Then I would rush back to my workplace and work until 5 pm. In the thirty minute break I had before starting overtime I would visit a few more nearby workplaces. I worked overtime from 5.30 pm until 8 pm. As soon as work was over I would head off to the Club's office. A lot of young people would be gathered there, printing out materials for various gatherings. We would do this together or have a meeting and before we knew it, it was midnight. I would rush to catch the last train, and when I arrived home and got to bed it was about 1.30 am. I would then be woken up again at 5.30 the next morning. I continued this life for several years. But it was not only me, numerous young people lived this life with a passion, and did so happily.

Since I completely ignored my home life and focused on activism, it is a wonder my family did not make a fuss. Shibata always emphasised: 'You must respect your family ... You are able to be activists because you have the support of your family. You must humbly interact with your family', which is, I think, the reason there was no resistance from them.

But in the midst of this activism, occasionally we would fall into a decline. Shibata was very attentive to such moments. When he thought we had fallen into a slump he would invite us for coffee or a movie. Listening to classical music at a cafe he would encourage us while explaining the meaning of the music. Or at the movies, whichever movie we were watching, he would find a lesson within it and provide strong encouragement. If he thought we looked tired, he would bring a novel to help cheer us up. He inspired us by making us read *How the Steel was Tempered* and *Virgin Soil Upturned*. Thanks to his care, the activists were able to get out of their depression quite quickly and energetically participate in activism once again.

Guidance for broadening the organisation

When I visited former Club members while writing this book, I asked them what kind of guidance they received from Shibata for dealing with organisational issues. Yoshimura [nee Sakurai] recalled the following.

> Shibata san told me never to leave work alone, to always go home with someone. That's when I was supposed to find out the complaints this person had in the workplace, and to bring them to the Club's office if possible. We were also taught to focus on important individuals when organising in target factories. For instance, in one factory, there was a worker who had the best skills in the company. The company based their piece rates on his speed. He was greatly trusted by the workers as well, thanks to his outstanding skills. When he suffered appendicitis, everyone in the Club actively supported him. As a result, he himself joined the Club, and thanks to him joining the Club, we managed to have a much larger presence at his workplace.

I also heard another incident, where a member once objected to letting an individual who was known to be a lazy worker join the Club. The member's argument was that it would be worthless to let someone like this person get involved. However, Shibata convinced him, arguing that what mattered was to capture new members through this individual.

When Watanabe Sei was setting up the Club's Women's Section, there was a female member who was known to be a delinquent. When Watanabe proposed that this member should leave the Club, Shibata answered:

> Even if she is a delinquent, you shouldn't think on the same level as she does. We need to make efforts to bring our friends back to the right path, so that we don't lose a single comrade. If we're not doing this, there's no point in being Club members.

Later, through the introduction of this delinquent member, we were fortunate enough to meet Nishida Tomiko, who became one of our core members. I heard so many episodes like this.

At that time, social clubs spontaneously emerged among Tokyo printworkers. Examples include Let's Work, which had exploited workers, a guild type organisation for European language printworkers that had a long history among printworkers, the Association of Japan Print Technicians, the New Skill Club and the Yokohama-based Bay Friendship Group. The reason behind the emergence of numerous social clubs was that printworkers had no other way of surviving than to get together and try to help each other out, since a lot of them were unemployed.

We considered unifying with all the other social clubs, except for Let's Work. Ideally, this proposal should come from the Club as we had the most members and were the most actively engaged and were therefore in the best position to approach other organisations. Between February and September 1937 we held eight meetings to discuss unification. Shiraishi, who was responsible for liaising with external organisations, displayed enormous capacity in moving this along. He worked to find the most conscious people within these organisations, and when he did he would meet them and encourage them to read. The discussions debated in these organisations included the following:

- to unite the job agency elements of each organisation
- to have a combined office
- to determine a minimum wage for the industry
- to publish a combined newsletter
- to hold a baseball game between each organisation.

Of these proposals, the only one that was achieved was the baseball matches, although, through these discussions the activists from the Association of Japan Print Technicians and the European language printers began to ask for guidance from the Club. In the middle of all this we continued to build, and held talks with *Kenseikai*, an organisation formed in Great Japan Printing, one of the larger printing companies, but without success.

9
Destruction of the union movement and formation of the PIA

The web of war collaboration

Japan's invasion of China continued to advance. The daily newspapers published maps of China and every time a city fell, they reported the news on the front page. When a large city surrendered, the government organised a lantern procession, trying to galvanise the citizens with 'We won, we won'. But the announcements from the imperial headquarters in actuality continued to deceive the population. The Chinese people's resistance, centred around the Chinese Communist Party, had prolonged this war over a long period. Chiang Kai Shek had withdrawn to a remote place in Chongqing. Japan, which could only secure pockets of the vast expanse of China, had to invest huge amounts of military personnel and goods. Among a section of the population a feeling of war weariness began to rise. Since the majority of the population was not told of the reality, they silently obeyed the military and the government.

Based on its National Personnel Mobilisation Law, the government established the Commodities Plan, which aimed to control all goods and labour for military demand. Using the slogan 'Luxury is the enemy' it introduced regulations banning the manufacture of luxury and non-urgent goods. As there was no petrol, cars ran on charcoal and firewood. Around the city, billboards constantly appeared with slogans such as 'No luxury for the real Japanese', and those which targeted women in included 'Let us stop having our hair permed' and 'Let us shorten our sleeves'.

Under the National Requisition Ordinance, workers like us, employed in non-military industries, were drafted into munitions factories by means of a letter from the government that was nicknamed the blue paper. The working population had to put up with all this in the name of the war.

When the overseas invasions reached a new level in June 1940, the Social Masses Party, which purported to be anti-capitalist, anti-fascist and anti-communist but in reality agreed with the war of invasion, dissolved itself. This was because the government put pressure on it, ordering it to change the party name because it was too class-based, and subsequently ordered it to disband, which it could no longer resist. At the disbanding ceremony the party paid homage to the imperial palace, the national anthem was sung, prayers were offered for the army's continued success in the war and a minute's silence was held for the war dead. In October, the Imperial Rule Assistance Association (IRAA) formed. It was based on the government bureaucracy; it had multiples branches in all areas and had private sector leaders serving as auxiliary bureaucrats. The government's purpose in creating the IRAA was to weave a web around the population to force their cooperation with the war.

Private sector independent organisations were forced to dissolve and were folded into the IRAA. The IRAA also formed neighbourhood associations at the local level, strengthening its structure. When we attended the regular meetings of the neighbourhood associations, those in charge who had connections with the police threw their weight around, ordering everyone to undertake activities such as collecting waste and unused items, cooperating in economising on rice [by not eating as much] or to be mobilised for a day of community cleaning, declaring that this was a public duty. They even made people carry out defence practice, and take buckets for extinguishing fires. People were also forced to donate for defence and buy government war bonds. Life simply became more and more painful. Eventually, the head of the neighbourhood association even observed our private life. Internationally, circumstances also became more strained and then, on the morning of the 1 September 1939, the German army invaded Poland marking the beginning of World War 2.

Shibata put a lot of effort into helping the activists understand these events. He often went to bookstores and, despite wartime conditions, if there were books that introduced the international context, without fail he would buy them. He grasped the character of China's Red Army through Agnes Smedley's *Travelling with the Eighth Route Army*. Through understanding how strongly it maintained military discipline, he finally came to believe that China would win in the end. He often told us about the Eighth Route Army. For activists who were influenced heavily by articles in the mainstream media, Shibata tried to convey the honest truth regarding the progress of the war in Germany and China.

By then, the war of invasion in China had developed into something more than a problem between Japan and China. The war was now wedged into the context of World War 2, which was a conflict between fascist and anti-fascist countries. In other words, the war had gone so far that even if Japan had wished for peace as a result of having had its fingers burnt in China, the conflict could not be resolved except on an international scale.

The military made a final big gamble. The previous year, 1939, the Japanese army had launched a war on the Soviet Union, aiming to strike the enemy's supply routes but was thoroughly crushed by the Soviet army. This time, in order to gain oil and other resources from the southern hemisphere, Japan plunged into war with the British, American, French and Dutch armies that surrounded Japan. To deal these countries a blow and to create a chance to make peace was the only way left for Japan to get out of the bog. In order to realise this, Japan needed to complete the repressive structure at home and to force the working class to cooperate to ensure the massive expansion in productive capacity needed to carry out the final stages of the war.

Organisation of the PIA

In 1939 the health and internal affairs vice-ministers released an instruction that forced the population to organise themselves into the PIA through government and private sector cooperation. The president of the PIA was also president of the Japan National Railway; the chair was the former internal affairs vice-minister. Other officials included Special Police, bureaucrats and those who managed labour affairs in the armaments industries, and the former Social Masses Party leadership. The Special Police forced the dissolution of trade unions throughout Japan to absorb them into this newly created government-sponsored organisation. Yamanashi, who liaised with the police on the Club's behalf, commented:

> From the time the Club office was created in Shiba, I carried out a role that was a kind of police liaison for the Club. My job was to deliver the meeting schedule of the head office and the Shiba branch each month to the police department and the local area command. After the meetings I would deliver a report detailing the content of the meetings and the number of attendees. Also I took a copy of the monthly newsletter to the police department's censorship section. This was a time consuming and unpleasant task. Because of this role I could never work long in any one workplace. On the day I had to deliver the materials I would be late for work or on occasions I had to take a day off from work.
>
> At the beginning of 1940 I received a demand from the local Special Police which read: 'The PIA is to be formed soon. Trade unions are to be dissolved into the PIA. How about your group joining the PIA like other unions?' He used the informal term for you, which was offensive. When I told Shibata he said, 'Just because they said this, there is no need to say "Yes, yes", and do what they ask. Let us consider the circumstances a little more.' So I drew it out a little longer, telling the police 'We are just a social group. I don't think we need to join the PIA. On top of that, each individual member is already a member of the PIA at their workplace.' The police, in the manner typical of the bureaucracy, seemed to think that they could have their way by acting in an intimidating manner. They repeated that we must dissolve the organisation and join the PIA. At first things took the form of an earnest request but finally it turned into threats: 'If you don't join the PIA, we'll lock up the entire leadership.'

Once it got to this stage it was no longer possible to feign ignorance. I responded: 'Either way, since we have to consult with everyone, we will respond by the end of this month. We would like you to wait until then', and went back to our office.

In what manner did the police carry out the Health and Internal Affairs Ministries' decision, forcing all of Japan's trade unions to dissolve? According to materials from the Ministry of Internal Affairs at least thirty-four unions with memberships of more than 1000 including communication employees, gas workers, electricity workers, transport workers and dockworkers disbanded during the year. The official statistics show that there were no trade unions in Japan from this time until the end of the war.

The largest remaining union, the GFL, tried to retain its organisation, but the two top leaders were called into police headquarters and threatened with a painful fate if they did not disband. Eventually, the GFL had to dissolve.

In these pressured circumstances, the state did not allow any unions to continue, not even the right wing conciliatory unions that collaborated with the state, so they also disbanded.

What was really lucky for the GFL leadership was that since it had held back from disbanding and subsequently was late in getting on the PIA bandwagon, they escaped being removed from government positions in the post-war period.

A thoroughgoing order to dissolve

On the basis of threats from the Health and Internal Affairs Ministries, the GFL disbanded, leaving behind a sorrowful statement. The order forcing the dissolution of trade unions under the pretty title of 'developmental dissolution' was thoroughgoing. It forced unions to dispose of all their assets, erasing even their last traces. The following gives a characteristic example.

Seafarers who had been members of a disbanded union in Hyōgo prefecture gathered together to erect a stone monument to commemorate their union on vacant land in front of the maritime union building. Learning of this, the Hyōgo prefecture Special Police stated that the underlying motive of the commemorative stone was to display permanently the class significance of the union as a class-oriented union. In view of where it was erected it would remind current and former seafarers of the union's consciousness. Based on this argument, the police made them re-inscribe the monument, changing the wording from Japan Seafarers Union Commemorative Stone to Japan Seafarers Building Commemorative Stone.

The Special Police intensified scrutiny of organisations, even after they disbanded. If police knew that former union members were holding a meeting, they would come and close it down.

The PIA was formed on the ruins of the union movement, on 23 November 1940. It organised 5.5 million workers and, while resembling a union, it was anything but a union. It was a bureaucratic mechanism for the massive wartime mobilisation of workers controlled by the health and internal affairs ministries. The PIA forced workers into military production and for capitalists it was a slave labour-like organisation that guaranteed unlimited exploitation. Thus the wartime structure was complete. In 1941 the Pacific War was about to begin.[33]

Shibata had expected the order to dissolve before it came, and commented that

> The right wing leadership of Japan's union movement cooperated with the military and wrecked the union movement. They sold out workers to the enemy. Because of this lots of organisations have been forced to disband. In time the order to disband will probably come to the Club as well. If we continue our activism in the way that we always have, we will be targeted as 'red'. We must continue the Club, no matter what it takes. We must continue our organisation, even if we have no choice but to take a form that looks like we have jumped on the bandwagon ourselves. As long as workers wish to stick together, class consciousness will increase. Let's not obsess about form. The choices left for us include shifting to an activism

---

33 Ohara Social Science Institute, Hōsei University, 1965, in *Taiheiyō Sensōka no Rōdō Undō (The Union Movement During the Pacific War)*: 43.

tied into daily life such as a consumer cooperative or a skills study group involving printing companies. Such organisations would be seen as necessary in everybody's eyes. We need to consider this point very carefully.

Thus he argued, and made everyone read the book on England's Rochdale community cooperatives, which started in 1844. We immediately started working hard to take the movement in this direction. We negotiated with a consumer cooperative to receive ration identification for charcoal so we could go north with a charcoal seller and buy charcoal. We bought two loads of charcoal, which we took back to Tokyo. One load was for the charcoal seller, the second load we distributed to our members in Shiba, Kanda, Kyōbashi and Fukagawa. Shiraishi, Sugiura and Taguchi helped out in the distribution using hand and bicycle drawn carts. In addition, many of us also helped out with repairing the paper screen doors in members' houses.

We also tried to establish a Skills Study Group to win over the workshop managers, our selling point being increasing the efficiency of the print industry, which was a handicraft industry. We met some managers with whom we discussed the design aspects of typesetting, among other topics. We put a lot of effort into this because we were trying to make a new legal organisation into which the entirety of the Club, as it was presently operating, could join and be endorsed by these employers. Shibata met with the chair of the Young Print Managers/Owners Federation. Kōmiya, who accompanied him, said that for Shibata, who was scrupulously honest, meeting with management over drinks was pretty intolerable.

As for the *haiku* and travel groups that we had been organising, we tried to continue them, not as purely entertainment activities but as part of the 'Make good use of your leisure hours' movement which was actively promoted by the Health Affairs ministry. This provided us with a cover and allowed us to minimise the scrutiny we faced from our enemies.

With a letter of introduction signed by his boss, Kōmiya visited the Tokyo City Labour Bureau to ask the Bureau section head to write an article about the Beach House showing how the project suited the current climate since it helped people put leisure hours to good use and to train their mind and body. The article was to be printed in the Club's newsletter. It was usually really hard to get someone from the Labour Bureau to write such articles. Kōmiya nearly gave up, but then Shibata said that 'You can write the article and get permission to publish it under the section head's name. We only need his job title.' In the end the section head grudgingly signed the article.

Meanwhile, Shibata had been taking thorough measures to ensure that the Club would survive, even when the order to disband came, in effect by preparing for the conversion to book, travel and *haiku* clubs.

Searching for a path to continue the Club

Shibata foresaw the repression. He spoke to a small number of leading activists and warned of the psychological preparedness needed.

> I don't think repression will come our way but I think it is still worthwhile considering what to do in case it comes. If you are locked up, you must absolutely not speak about organisational matters. For example, if you think of telling the police something because you want to get hit eight times instead of ten, that is the end for all of us. Nothing is small enough that you can tell the police without putting other people in danger. You have to understand that, however small a thing you tell them, someone will be locked up. Therefore, it's crucial to keep in mind that you are to say absolutely nothing. If you have class hatred, you can withstand any amount of violence. You must fight with confidence in that every bit of violence you endure, a person who will take on the next generation will be born.

One Sunday at the end of August 1940, more than thirty people gathered at the Beach House. It was a meeting to decide to continue the Club. The basic direction had already been decided at a meeting at Shibata's house. The leading activists had stayed the night before and developed the plan. The reason we had as many as thirty people there was because we had organised a mobilisation beforehand, asking the activists to come with certain people. A journalist from Dōmei Press was also present. He was not formally attending, as we set it up as if he just coincidentally happened to be there. We asked him to speak about the international situation. I do not remember whether the journalist left right after his talk or remained.

> Finally, Shibata proposed the direction that had been decided on beforehand.
>
> I have no desire to see the Club disappear. If it disappears, workers who need solidarity will have nothing to support them. Will they have the PIA? That is an organisation that uses workers as instruments of war. It is just a top down organisation, it does not allow any worker-to-worker connections. I want the Club to remain for these workers. We have to take on the role of connecting workers from each workplace. My feeling has been decided well beforehand. We gathered everyone to hear each other's thoughts and I understand that generally everyone has the same opinion.
>
> But even though we say we want the Club to remain, it cannot remain as it is now. So, let us disband, on the surface, as is desired by the police. But if we separate off the jobs that the Club is doing now to operate independently, in effect the Club can still remain. For example, the travel section can become a travel club. The *haiku* section becomes a *haiku* club, and the book section becomes a book club. Club members can become members of the various clubs. This way we can maintain the current organisation. As for contact between the various clubs, we will do it with caution. To a certain extent this path is dangerous, but no movement is without danger. Shall we do it?

Following what was decided with the previous night's preliminary discussions, someone raised their voice in approval and thus it was decided. This decision to covertly continue our activism was extremely important. It was an act of resistance against the policy of the state. The state at this point had reached an impasse with the war in China and was plunging into war with the USA and Britain in order to break this stalemate. State policy was to completely smash all unions. Our actions were going to resist this direction. Shibata couldn't have decided to continue the Club in an unplanned manner without considering the context. Had the circumstances allowed, the best way would have been to explain the situation to all attendees to clarify what might happen if people voted for the Club to continue. This would allow them to mentally prepare themselves to fight the coming repression and to voluntarily decide what they would do. But if he had spoken frankly people might have voted against continuation of the Club. I imagine that Shibata agonised over this dilemma and that he hoped from the bottom of his heart that there would be no repression. Throughout all the activities that followed, he put his life on the line and fought to the end.

When I reflect on this time now, although I was subject to repression, was arrested and imprisoned, I think that the decision of this meeting to continue the Club and not obey the government's order to disband, was the correct one. Other activists who also participated in the Beach House meeting are today active in the union movement or in other areas of democratic activity for the development of democratic print works, which are workshops that print JCP and other left wing groups' materials. I believe all these other members would look back at Shibata's decision as the correct one.

Since the meeting was run in this way, few among the participants were aware that the continuation of the Club was something that would definitely, if revealed to the police, amount to the arrests of all those present. We also felt relatively at ease since so far we had been able to develop our activism with little trouble.

The beginning of covert activism

The Club's dissolution ceremony, which occurred simply for form's sake, took place at the Club's head office with the local Special Police in attendance. A participant recalls the situation of that time:

> A lot of the activists, including Shiraishi, were at the dissolution

ceremony. There was a strange man in a suit who belonged to the Special Police who ordered Shiraishi to write down the names of all those in attendance. Looking at everyone's face, Shiraishi wrote all the names, handed over the document to the guy, and then it was over. After the ceremony Shiraishi called out to me, 'Let's go home together'; we went from Shinbashi to Ginza. Goods were in short supply because of the intensifying war and shop windows were quite empty. Shiraishi said he was looking to buy butter and cheese for his wife, who was pregnant. After that we went into a coffee shop in Ginza. There Shiraishi fixed his eyes on my face and told me, as if trying to calm me: 'The names of attendees I wrote down were all false. I did not write down your name.' There was little I could say. That was because I could not find the right words to offer to Shiraishi sitting in front of me who, completely different from his usual, cheerful self, looked painfully downcast.

From this point on, Shiraishi withdrew from Club activity for the rest of the war. I do not know why.

It became increasingly hard to organise even cultural groups. Even churches which refused to state that they were representing a 'genuine Japanese Christianity' [as opposed to a western import] became the focus of repression. In August 1940, many local theatre groups were repressed, their members were arrested and finally they were forced to disband. Such control over working people's lives and the harsh repression were all for war purposes.

The military, which had been driven into a situation in which it could only hold small areas in the vast regions of China, was extremely nervous. On the pretext of cutting the enemy's supply lines, it extended the war front to India and Burma, and then, due to the economic blockade by Britain, the USA and the Netherlands, penetrated further to Indochina, the Philippines, Borneo, Sumatra, New Guinea and Australia in the hunt for resources. On top of that, it was preparing to further mobilise the population in preparation for war with the USA and Britain.

In the midst of these increasingly dark conditions Club members worked behind the back of the Special Police to recover contact with workplaces.

Each branch established its own travel and *haiku* clubs, and as the means to connect the respective clubs a simple library was established at Shibata's place. The activity was no different from before apart from the fact that all Club members could not get together to do things as one group.

The activities went well. Some travel clubs started a monthly instalment system for travel expenses. At times, two travel clubs would organise joint activities. When recruiting members, however, we worked separately.

Covert activities

Around this time the government, which had gone all out in support of Germany, introduced hiking and recreational activities similar to the Nazi *Wandervögel* youth organisations. In Germany, as a means of cohering youth, the Nazis made them live together and travel in big organised groups. They were mobilised for labour under slogans such as 'Work is joy'. Two of the Club's travel clubs, posing as advocates of *Wandervögel*, mobilised young people from many workplaces for mountain climbing.

During the outings we would hold a big get together at the top of the mountains where we ate with people who we met for the first time, cooked miso soup, discussed issues that arose at our workplaces, sang songs, performed tricks and generally had a good time. While climbing down the mountain we even sang May Day songs. By doing all this, we maintained the connections between members. We made efforts to keep the former Club members close and to preserve the organisation of printworkers.

One participant recalls the activities of the time.

> I became the person responsible for one of the *haiku* clubs. But of course, *haiku* was not my sole responsibility. I helped with the travel and ran around carrying books for the book clubs. It was not only me; everyone else did the same thing. The people responsible for each of the clubs were separated on the surface so that they would not have the same name or address, but at their roots, all of the clubs were firmly connected.

The shift to the new organisation went comparatively well, and I think most of the former Club members were included. The *haiku* club especially developed well and we were able to organise new people. In doing things, whether *haiku* or anything else, we always drew new people into the organisation. With the *haiku* magazine two workers at different workplaces took turns to provide the cover art. We had a lot of people help us with all the process of magazine making, including the manuscripts, plate making, binding, and distribution, through which we became much closer. We printed about 300 copies of the magazine and would hand them out to readers, even if they were not eager to submit their works. The most important thing, however, was that the magazine linked us to many readers in various workplaces. It was a tool for connecting workplaces as readers would often recommend it to others in workplaces where we had not yet made contact.

We would hold a *haiku* gathering every two or three months. Since prizes of food and other necessities were awarded, it was always well attended and had a good reputation. The attendees were all printworkers and typesetters, so, quite naturally, they would talk about the situation in their workshops, enabling us to understand the lives and actions of workers in the factories.

Avoiding the eye of the police

One member commented on the activities that occurred after the shift to the new organisational structure.

After becoming a travel club we went to the mountains often. We, the activists, were ourselves so taken by the beauty of mountains that we even began to dream of climbing in winter. We would leave on Saturday night and come back Sunday night. This schedule was so convenient for young people like us that sometimes we went on hikes every week. We would never climb alone however. Even when going in small groups we would always invite people who were helpful with our activism or other young people to come along.

We organised an easy hiking trip to Mt Jimba and Kobotoke Pass as a combined event for all three travel clubs of Kanda, Kyōbashi and Shiba. I guess about fifty people attended. Some new members joined in the course of preparation for this event. Also, during the hike, we encouraged these people to work proactively and care for the participants. We climbed Mt. Fuji as a group as well.

I think it was early summer, I had collected the books for book club readers from the bookshelf on the second floor of Shibata's house and was on my way home. Suddenly I was stopped by a cop at a police station near Kinshichō station and was questioned about what I was doing. I was startled since it was so sudden and also it was the first time for me to be questioned. I did as asked and undid my *furoshiki* [large cloth used for carrying parcels] to show the cop what was inside. There were a lot of books, probably including titles like The *Ecology of Marriage* by Ishikawa Tatsuzō and *Tajinko Village*, and it was incredibly bulky. He asked, 'What are you doing with so many books?' I replied, 'It is for a reading club. These are for the members.' The cop just grunted and that was it. As I was climbing the stairs to the platform of Kinshichō station, there was a sharp-eyed looking detective. It was only then that I realised they had formed a chain because of some incident.

The next day, I spoke to Kōmiya and to Shibata. They listened carefully to what I had to say and then said: 'It was probably a mistake to say it was for a book club. That cop probably did not understand, but book clubs are used by political groups fairly often as an excuse and if it had been a Special Police they would have understood straight away.'

I felt completely dejected. But Shibata said to me, 'Don't worry too much. From now on you should take more care', and then he changed the subject. From that time on I bought canvas shoes and for example wore hiking clothes, to avoid suspicion.

Taguchi recalls that when he carried books for the book club, he would dress in mountain climbing gear and carry the books in a backpack to deceive police.

Even during the darkness of wartime, no matter how much the government increased the repression, the dissatisfaction with the war spread among those living at the bottom of society. There were endless instances of people making antiwar remarks at meetings or distributing dangerous literature to vent their stress. These cultural activities carried over into the next year.

Although we were conducting these activities with the purpose of increasing solidarity, some of the activists got caught up in the organisational tactics. They were captivated by the allure of the mountains and forgot that the important task was to build the organisation.

The Club's Women's Section continued in the midst of severe repression

Only the Club's Women's Section remained as it was. At first, Kōmiya and Taguchi, who oversaw the Women's Section, thought of disbanding it and including it in the travel clubs. When they consulted with Shibata he offered his view:

> I think you need to think it over. The status of women in present day Japan is extremely low. On top of that, the current situation is that even when they are active, they are not noticed at all. So from this perspective, it is best to maintain the Women's Section as it is. We can come up with a name that does not really draw attention. The term 'Yamato Nadeshiko'[34] that was proposed in your discussion is a popular term right now, so why not put this suggestion forward? The

---

34 Term used to describe a Japanese woman with all the traditional graces or the epitome of Japanese womanhood. Yamato is the ancient name for Japan and a *nadeshiko* is a type of carnation.

problem is the content. Make it worker-oriented and all will be good.

Kōmiya and Taguchi gathered the women together and consulted them and from this the *Nadeshiko Mustumi Kai* (Nadeshiko Friendship Association) was founded.

The core of the Women's Section was Nishida Tomiko, Mizuno, Yagi plus others. They published a twelve to sixteen page mimeographed newsletter. The group had about sixty women members, who continued through the most brutal repression; they went hiking, held cooking classes and discussed plays. Mizuno Shizue, spoke of those times.

> Even now, I remember Shibata's words. He said, 'Born into this world, human beings have the responsibility to do something for society. No matter how much you improve yourself, unless everyone is better off, you cannot say that the world has become a better place.'
>
> A sense of accomplishment was important in our life. We felt that we were living our lives to the fullest. But if I am honest, I remember that being active was difficult. It used up our time, there were no Sundays or holidays. During lunch times, we would ring up members at our own expense. Every night I would get home after 11 pm. My mother would frequently scold me and tell me that she would disown me. Nishida and I talked about quitting the Club many times. We decided that as soon as we got our wages, we would give the bulk of it to our families. Although our families said they would disown us, they really believed that their daughters were not doing anything wrong. It was difficult being an activist but we could bear this because of the lessons of the Club. If I think about the situation of the time, we were living our lives with all our might. I have no regrets over my youth.

This kind of activism was never easy during the war because whatever activism you did, you were watched by the Special Police. Thinking about that, it is almost miraculous that we were able to continue doing it for so long.

10
Difficulties we faced during the period of covert activity

The dramatic decline in membership

We continued the diverse activities of the Club for a year and a half after it 'disbanded'. When we say continued, it was different to operating legally. With all the restrictions that accompanied the repression, our membership numbers drastically declined. Also, starting with Kōmiya, one after another our core activists were conscripted. In addition, since the print industry was deemed non-essential and non-urgent during wartime, workers were drafted into the munitions industry. One by one activists were drafted into the military factories which was a severe blow to our organisation.

The Club's practice became as unstable as a small boat being washed away by a strong current. The decline in members led to a situation where we would not be able to be active without securing someone in a permanent position, which required funds. It was important not to scatter the Club's core members. With Shibata at the centre, we planned to secure our income by undertaking the management of Meibunsha, a print works that was to be closed because of financial difficulties. Through an introduction from a member's father, Shibata negotiated with the owner and reached an agreement to take over the management. The profits were to be shared proportionately between the owner and the workers. In this workplace we gathered together a number of former Club leaders.

Since the majority of leaders were now working in the same workplace, it was much easier to communicate with each other. But since work became really busy, we struggled to secure time for our activism. From early in the morning until late at night everyone worked extremely hard. A workplace where workers had direct control over production was like a dream. We thought if we worked hard enough, we could free up one person to be an activist full-time.

Our print works had to take on jobs that were incompatible with our members' ideology. Though it could not be helped, because it was war time, we had to pick and set type for a right wing magazine. We did not really appreciate doing this kind of job, but it was the best kind of workplace to escape the eye of the Special Police. We activists tried not to be choosy about the jobs.

The only proper client we had was Mikasa Shōbo, a major publishing company. We printed *A Moonflower in Heaven* by Nakagawa Yoichi for this company; it became a bestseller. We also took on subcontract work for three print works in Kyōbashi, where other members were employed. Everyone put in a lot of effort to make the running of this print works a success. Every day Shibata worked at carrying out the jobs more efficiently so that as many people as possible could spend time on some aspect of activism. For this reason when the manuscripts came in he would thoroughly examine the contents in order to make the job easier. As a result of our improving methods, there is no doubt that our efficiency also rapidly increased.

All these efforts were in the face of ever increasing pressure. Tōjō Hideki, a hardliner who said 'Sometimes it is necessary for us to close our eyes and jump off the deep end', was given an imperial mandate to form a cabinet. He plunged us into a war with the USA.

The radio broadcast the news. 'Before dawn on 8 December, the Imperial Navy entered into war with the US and the British forces in the West Pacific.' Three hundred and fifty planes from the Japanese Navy had attacked Pearl Harbour, sinking six out of eight ships of the US Pacific Fleet and destroying 164 warplanes. On 8 December 1941 the population listened to the imperial edict declaring the start of the war; *Kimi ga Yō*, the national anthem, was played.

Immediately, the war effort moved southward and was declared 'successful beyond expectations'. The war front had extended to Malaya [as it then was], Singapore and Sumatra. Through the expanded war, the population was driven into even deeper gloom than before.

The day after hostilities began, the government introduced emergency measures. Early on the morning of 9 December it proceeded to order the arrest the 'dangerous people' it had previously been watching. In total 496 people were arrested.[35]

Not long after, the Temporary Directive on Speech, Publication and Association was enacted. With this, political freedom, which had already been severely restricted, was fundamentally removed.

Parting from Shibata

The activism based at Meibunsha continued, but here I must talk about an enormous personal change that happened to me. While working at Meibunsha, for the first time ever I disobeyed Shibata who I respected more than anyone else, and eventually ended up leaving the company. This wasn't an ideological conflict; it was purely work related.

Our conflict began when we started to work on our own at Meibunsha, we realised we could not possibly survive by simply relying on existing customers. We desperately needed to find new customers. I was transferred to the sales department. This was something that could be described as an exceptional promotion, but as I had been trained as a type picker I found my new job difficult. I just could not bring about good results. This must have been frustrating for Shibata who was working so hard to put the company on track. One day in February 1942, he shouted at me without hearing my side. Being told off in front of many co-workers upset me and, without saying a word, I went straight back home. I then missed several days without leave. Shibata did not come to visit me, probably to teach me a lesson. That made it too difficult for me to apologise. After some time, Shibata sent Nishida Tomiko, head of the Club's Women's Section, to check on me in a very casual manner. That made me all the more stubborn. I kept

---

35 *Shakai Undō no Jōkyō 1941 (The State of Social Movements 1941)* v13: 235–6

saying that I was quitting Meibunsha without listening to a word she said.

In the midst of all this, I made the mistake of starting work at a print works in Hongō. In this way, I was responsible for deepening the rift between myself and Shibata. Having distanced myself from comrades with whom I had worked for so long, I suffered daily from despondency. My conscience whispered to me that I had dropped out from the struggle. I had been someone who worked hard as an activist night and day, but then, all of a sudden, I was no longer an activist. My daily life consisted of coming back from work and reading, and occasionally going to the movies when I felt too lonely. Nishida continued to visit me. As we were young, we became close and eventually decided to marry.

Nishida insisted that we convey our marriage to Shibata so that he would acknowledge it and I agreed. Secretly, I felt that having Shibata recognise our marriage would lead to being forgiven.

He was overjoyed for us. Two or three days later, we heard from him that he was also thinking of getting the two of us together. In May 1942 we married. I should have visited Meibunsha to apologise to my colleagues using the pretext of our marriage. But in August, while I was hesitating, the first round of arrests of Club members occurred. Shibata and Shiraishi were the first to be taken. Later, while Shibata and I were both in Yokohama prison, Shibata talked to me affectionately for the first time since our separation, making me feel that I was finally forgiven. On that day, having met accidentally in the bath house and away from the eyes of the guard, we exchanged a heartfelt handshake.

With unions forcibly disbanded, workers did not have the means to protect their rights or livelihoods with the power of solidarity. On the contrary, under the pretext that it was a state of emergency, workers had to work under the eye of the Special Police, believing that the war would end in victory. We had to carry a work pass, we could not change workplaces, wages were held down by wage control regulations, rice was rationed and clothing was regulated through a stamp system. The price of black market goods continued to increase. The only tactic left to workers was to submit petitions to their companies.

Workers' resistance spontaneously turned to sabotage. Statistics for

1942 from the Ministry of Internal Affairs, noted:

- an increase in people arriving late or leaving work early
- an increase in absenteeism; the national average was between 12 and 30 per cent but in July, 94 per cent of the workforce in one factory in Okayama was absent
- workers absconded from companies they were drafted into
- workers moved around to different factories, even illegally in a significant number of cases
- an increase in the number of workers working two jobs, for example, they would leave one workplace at 4 pm without overtime and in the evening, after eating dinner, at 5.30 pm, would go to work at a neighbourhood factory until 5 am the next day, then going back to the first workplace at 7 am; since this worker worked an all night shift at the factory, he would sabotage his work and, in some cases, would disappear to take a nap in the store room
- a national increase in work stoppages; if a supervisor was present they would work, but if absent they would not; a number of workers would make personal items during work time
- a significant increase in cases of worker misbehaviour, including burglary inside and outside workplaces either solo or in groups, stealing, assaults, fraud, intimidation, open gambling at workplaces, misbehaviour of trainee and drafted workers
- an increase in collective violence against supervisors and management.[36]

---

36 *Shakai Undō no Jōkyō 1942 (The State of Social Movements 1942)* v14: 407

11
Successive repression

In the early stages of the war, most people thought that Japan was winning. In reality, the state of the war was increasingly serious. The Japanese military suffered a massive defeat in the Battle for Midway and the aircraft carriers that were the Japanese navy's 'cherished treasures', were hit and sunk by the US military's counterattack.

On 18 April 1942, enemy aircraft began bombing attacks on the main island of Honshu. Bombs were dropped on Tokyo, Kanagawa, Aichi, Hyōgo and so the population got a taste of how serious things could be.

On 30 April 1942 there was a general election. The IRAA endorsed 467 candidates, most of whom were elected. But it was clear that many people had severe criticisms of this election. The following comments were scribbled on ballot papers:[37]

- The government is our enemy, what are small business owners to do?
- A bonus of miso and soy sauce please
- You cannot fight on an empty stomach
- The soldiers' code is don't eat, don't drink, just work
- Rice instead of elections
- Crushing us the powerless in the name of maintenance while

---

37 *Shakai Undō no Jōkyō 1942 (The State of Social Movements 1942)* v14: 520.

letting the bureaucrats and big business owners gain? What a huge arsehole, sack Tōjō
- Wages are low, life is tough, they say elections yet things are rough.

The election was uncritically backed by all factions. Eighty-five independents were elected; however, those candidates who had professed to be representatives of workers but actually cooperated with the war effort were defeated.

During all of this the leaders of the Club continued their activism with Meibunsha as their mainstay. But I now think that in these dangerous circumstances it was natural that our activism was soon exposed.

In August 1942 Shibata and Shiraishi were arrested by Kanagawa police. Fujisaka, who oversaw the offset printworkers, recalls how the arrests began.

> I spoke with Shibata and we started to extend our organising among offset printers. One of the young offset printers handed out antiwar leaflets around Yokohama harbour and that became the pretext that enabled the police to take 14 others, including Shibata, from Tokyo to Yokohama.

We too believed in this story, but while studying many documents to write this book, I found the following record in *Shakai Undō no Jōkyō 1942 (The State of Social Movements 1942)* by the Police Affairs Bureau, Ministry of Internal Affairs.

The situation surrounding the Hiratsuka group incident

The arrests

> In Kanagawa, the seven individuals listed below have been arrested since 28 February: Takanashi Shigeharu (35), Sasaya Jirō (33), Shibata Ryūichirō (35), Shiraishi Mitsuo (31), Imamura Tadayori (37), Fujisaka Fusao (40), Gomi Norio (34).

Their activism

> From around October 1931, Takanashi Shigeharu has been in communication with JCP members such as Azuma Shigeo and Fukuie Susumu and became a candidate for party membership. Since then, he has been working on expanding the party membership in the Shōnan Hiratsuka area where he was arrested. In April 1930, as a special consideration, his indictment was suspended at Yokohama District Court, but he did not change his communist beliefs and covertly maintained communication with his comrades ... In April 1937, he joined the Club, whose core members were Shibata Ryūichirō and Shiraishi Mitsuo. There, he engaged in activism such as publishing the organisation's newsletter *Club News* to promote class consciousness among its readership, as well as infiltrating progressive elements into targeted workplaces to induce strikes.
>
> Later, in April 1939, he temporarily went back home to Hiratsuka for recuperation, but, enthused by the social situation of 1940–41, as well as conditions such as the food shortage, he regained his interest in activism. After communicating and discussing with his comrade Sasaya Jirō, he concluded that preparation must be made for an armed insurrection in the whole of the Hiratsuka area in response to the proletarian revolution that was to come in the near future. To this end, he formed the Hiratsuka group and worked to equip said group for its purpose.
>
> As stated above, the Hiratsuka group was formed with the intention of starting an armed insurrection, but it also intended to start an armed insurrection in the Hiratsuka area, taking advantage of the confusion during air raids in the context of the Japan–USA–Britain war.

As stated in this document, this incident was most likely the trigger for our arrests.

Those working in Meibunsha continued their daily jobs while visiting the imprisoned people to give them necessities. There also were signs that made us expect a second round of arrests, such as the appearance of a strange rag collector repeatedly walking into the alley in front of Meibunsha during lunchtime when everybody was gathered together.

From 11 November, a second round of arrests occurred and seven of us, including me, were arrested, while many others were taken in for questioning. One of those arrested recounted:

> It was the morning of 11 November. When I got to the entrance of the workshop five or six minutes late, there was a strange commotion. Two or three plain clothes police immediately surrounded me. Inside the factory, I silently exchanged glances with Taguchi, who was also surrounded by two or three plain clothes cops. We nodded to each other, then we were taken outside.

Kawasaki, a Club member, took over the reins of Meibunsha and became key to managing it. He soon went off to fight. With the successive arrest of the top leaders, the movement fell into a state of destruction. The workshop continued, managed by a core of women members.

Not only did those arrested suffer, but their families did as well. Some wives and mothers had no one to rely on and they asked people at Meibunsha for help. The Club members tried to help financially or by trying to find jobs. Also, we would go hiking in the countryside to try to obtain some vegetables or invite them to go to the beach to provide some recreation.

More workers from Meibunsha were drafted into war industries. As business generally continued to wind up, printing jobs disappeared and our print workshop eventually had to close. The women of Meibunsha went to work in a print works in Shiba. Since this workshop was suffering from labour shortages due to many of its workers being drafted into war industries, these women were enthusiastically welcomed.

Horrific torture

I was arrested in the second round up on the morning of 17 November.

At the time I was a temporary worker. My wife had gone to work but we had not told the landlord where she worked. The Special Police searched my family's home and that of my wife. My wife's family told her the Special Police had come, and then she rang me. I went straight home where I hid the most conspicuous books. After that I went to my wife's family home and had dinner.

Two Special Police arrived while I was there and arrested me. I was taken to Yokohama's Kanagawa Police station. The Special Police, who had been polite on the journey, completely changed their attitudes once we got to the police station. They took me to a martial arts training hall where five cops with wooden sticks and bamboo swords surrounded me. They started beating me wildly, grabbing me by the hair and dragging me around, hitting my knees with the wooden sticks, hitting my head with the bamboo swords, kicking my legs while forcing me to kneel on my haunches and standing on top of my legs as I was seated, threatening me with even worse violence. They said to me:

> You scum, joining the communists to turn Japan red in these times of emergency. What on earth are you thinking? Beating you to death would never be enough. Soldiers of the Imperial Army are fighting so hard to protect Japan at this very moment, in China and in the south. Have you even thought about that? Ever? You despicable traitors. Nobody would ever blame us if we kill two or three of you fucking lot. Be prepared, we'll beat you to death.

They kept this up for about two hours. This was my baptism on the first day of being locked up. When I was led to the cell, I was in no state to walk. Holding on to the Special Police's shoulder, I just made it. But the other detainees were very kind. They made me take off my trousers and looked at my knees, which were purple and swollen. They sympathised with me; everyone said 'What a cruel thing to do'. I was not questioned the next day or the day after that, but on the fourth day I was pulled along to the hall again. They dragged me around by my hair, beat me with bamboo swords, took turns stamping on my knees while I was sitting on my haunches, jumping up and down on my knees and kicking me, and repeating this cycle countless times.

I gathered while I was being tortured that a large number of Club members had been arrested. The Kanagawa prefectural police were very mobile, torturing detained members for information, then using the information to threaten other Club members. It was hell for those who were imprisoned. One after another new 'facts' arose. The Special Police even made up stories that suited their needs.

Later I heard that Shibata faced this violence with a solid determination, refusing to give in even a little. Whatever the Special Police asked him, whatever violence they inflicted on him, he was always calm and composed. He responded with:

> I am a communist. Telling me to abandon communism is the same as telling me to die. I don't need you telling me that you would kill me, for I have resolved to happily die for this belief. I have absolutely nothing to tell you. You can do whatever you like.

This attitude was common to many of the activists and the Kanagawa prefectural police were at a loss as to how to deal with it. Many of the leaders who had regularly heard the advice from Shibata about what to do in the case of arrest, resisted very well, although some did not.

For the 18 months I was in Kanagawa police detention, I began to see more and more detainees who were gaoled because of offences specifically created by the war conditions. Every day, people from various social classes came and went: teachers who had carelessly spoken out about their antiwar beliefs at school were pulled in because their students reported them, workers who committed sabotage were arrested; Christian clergy were arrested on suspicion of spying, people who were selling sewing needles were charged with contravening orders regulating commodities, and shipping industry bosses were involved in a major bribery scandal. These were all incidents that, in peace time, would not constitute crimes, but in the context of war there were stiff penalties.

I do not mean to say that I enjoyed other people's misfortune, but for us prisoners the comings and goings of these people was fortunate, as from their conversations we could grasp little by little what was happening to Japan.

A Kawasaki steel worker, who was pulled in for being absent without notice, told us that the German army was surrounded at Stalingrad and 350,000 of their soldiers had been annihilated by the Soviet army. Many of the detainees probably had only been taught that the German army was strong. They were astonished: 'The German army lost? That can't be true. It must be a mistake.' I thought, though, that the inevitable had happened and the impact on Japan would be significant.

After this turning point, the international situation changed. The offensive of the Allied forces was supported by the international working class, but this bright first dawn light had not yet reached Japan's working class. Despite the Pacific war edging closer and closer towards defeat, with General Yamamoto's death in action, and the 'death in honour' [complete destruction] of the Japanese army at the Battle of Attu and Kisuka Islands, the military responded with 'The war is severe' in order to tighten their grip over the social and political structure and further mobilise the population for war.

The previously voluntary labour service of students became compulsory. They were taken to work in arsenals, munitions factories and rural villages to needlessly fight in a war that there was no chance of winning. Their youth was trampled upon.

After questioning by the police was finished, the major figures among the Club members were sent to Yokohama Prison. Prison life continued for another six months.

Sometimes, when there was a judicial inquiry, we were taken blindfolded by car to the courthouse. The city, visible from chinks in the transport vehicle on our way there and back, was dramatically different. Men wore the national uniform complete with gaiters and a field service cap, women wore a hood to protect them from air raids and indigo died cotton pants suits. Even in prison such sights helped me feel the harshness of Japan's war time situation.

12
The approaching defeat

Conditions inside the gaol

Between May and October 1944 decisions were made about our sentences. Shibata, Taguchi and I were sent to prison; Shiraishi was released. Shibata was sentenced to seven years hard labour, while Taguchi and I were given three year sentences. Shiraishi was given a two year suspended sentence. Shiraishi was a key person in the Club but I think he received a suspended sentence because he did not participate in the covert activities.

The documents containing Shibata, Taguchi and my judgements were all destroyed by fire during the war but Shiraishi's was spared.[38]

While Shibata was absent, the Yagi family, who had escaped arrest, visited and supported his family. My mother and sisters protected my pregnant wife and assisted in the birth of our child. Taguchi's father, who was seriously depressed, was supported by Nakajima, who also helped him find some work. Things were tough not only for those imprisoned, but also for the families.

During this period counterattacks by the US army became more and more brutal each day. Even in prison the atmosphere of defeat was obvious. At exercise time, rumours flew around that the bells and pots of

---

38 Due to the fire bombings on Tokyo and other places, there are very few photos and memorabilia from the Club days. Shiraishi's sentencing document, which can be seen in the photo section, is one of the few remaining items.

temples had been taken in order to manufacture arms. It appeared that the shortage of goods was becoming even worse. The guards would say, 'You lot are lucky. We can only eat one bowl of noodles', but the wardens did take whatever they could from the prisoners' meals by demanding their rice. The food for prisoners gradually deteriorated: what was once rice and wheat became rice and soybeans, then rice and lumps of corn. The biggest treat had been the weekly tempura, even if it was just a single piece of deep fried vegetable. This then became extremely rare but varieties of seaweed became common and one day a week we would get only one pickled plum. Only at new year did we get one slice of the special new year food, which consisted of dried sticky rice made into squares and one mandarin. It was the sole pleasure.

Our clothes also became threadbare. The rule was that in winter we were supposed to receive a padded garment, but we never got this. In the middle of freezing January, at night with a cold wind blowing outside, in our unheated cells made of concrete with a wooden floor, we were clothed in a thin cotton shirt, a rayon jumper, trousers to our knees and no socks. In these conditions, the cold was the biggest danger. With poor food and barely any clothing, we started collapsing one after the other.

The deteriorating conditions meant that Japan's capacity to continue the war was pretty close to reaching its limit. Even we prisoners could see this reality. There were restrictions on lighting and the air raid siren would sound every night. When I looked outside the prison window, the sky towards Yokohama was bright red. Several planes were caught up in the fighting. I saw several planes crash but at first I did not know if they were friend or enemy. I remember it had a certain beauty, like watching a movie. But with repeated air raids, I clearly understood that fewer of Japan's planes were being sent out. Only the searchlights were vainly sending out beams of light. We could see that Japan no longer had the strength to engage enemy planes.

At this time, the guards overseeing us began to disappear one by one. When we asked why, the prisoner who assisted them he told us that they had been conscripted and sent to the war zone. The conditions in the Pacific war had become more pressing and anyone and everyone was being conscripted. Even students had their deferment cancelled. By the end of 1944, the war situation had become absolutely hopeless.

Reunion with Shibata

I had one happy occurrence while imprisoned. Although it was very brief, I was reunited with Shibata in a meeting that took place in the prison bath house; we were able to grasp each other's hands. About two and a half years had passed since we had seen each other. On that day, which was the once weekly bath day, prisoners in solitary confinement were taking a bath in the break from work. As usual, on the guard's order, we left our cell, formed a single line and headed towards the bath house. Here I will explain just a little about the bath house.

It was about the width of a 25 metre pool. At the entrance you would undress and place your clothes in boxes on a wooden shelf. When you left you were supposed to take your clothing from the other side of the shelf. Beyond this area was the first bath tub, and past that was the washing area.[39] Then came the second bath tub and beyond that were the sinks. A guard would be stationed in the centre and another with a wooden sword would keep an eye on the bathers. When the guards blew their whistle the twenty prisoners using the first bath tub would get out and proceed to the washing area and those in the washing area would proceed to the second bath tub. Those in the second bath tub would get out and head to the sink area and those at the sink would head to the dressing area to get dressed. At each whistle, each group would move. There was two minutes between each whistle, which hardly provided us enough time to get warm from the bath.

As everyone is naked when they are in the bath house, nobody would really notice who got together in the same bath tub. On that day, quite by accident, the bath times for Shibata, Taguchi and myself coincided. The

---

39 The first bath tub was probably to get wet in preparation for washing because there may not have been individual taps as there are now. In Japanese public bathing areas it is practice to completely wash and rinse oneself, including washing one's hair, before soaking in the bath tub. Japanese baths are like small plunge pools: the water is filled to about 1 metre deep and heated. The point is to soak in the tub for as long as you like to warm up and relax your muscles.

three of us instinctively gathered together. Facing the front guard and putting Shibata between us the three of us managed to grasp each other's hands. Shibata broke into a smile and briefly said to us, 'Are you well? Take care of yourself and get out of here soon.' I was so overwhelmed with emotion that I was nearly in tears. I believe Taguchi felt the same.

Throughout that day after the bath, even while working in my cell, I had a feeling of thorough satisfaction.

I guess at this point Shibata knew that the end of the war was drawing close. He wrote a letter to his mother and sister suggesting what he might do after his release:

> Here is my second letter to you from prison. How are you enduring the bombings? Since it's getting colder, spending time in the air-raid shelters will be tougher for you mother. Please fix the sleeves of my jumper so that you can wear it and keep warm. Also, how about making protective clothing using my coat? No need to be sparing, go ahead and make use of any of my personal belongings, my clothes or my undershirts. After you have done everything possible, just stay calm and try not to worry too much. No matter how much you worry, bombs will drop on you if they're supposed to. And if they're not supposed to, even if you're having fun, nothing will happen. Think of this as a chance to learn that 'Man proposes, God disposes.'
>
> To make daily life more interesting, once spring comes, use all the empty boxes and pots you can find to grow vegetables, just like we did last spring. I'd also suggest growing some flowers as well. Being able to watch red and green buds growing out of the ground gives joy and energy to our daily lives. Mother, you know very well about such joy. I suggest you start preparing the soil we need for this, even if only a bit at a time.
>
> Also, I remember you wrote to me in the last letter that you still have some of the spare money I saved up. Please use it to buy lottery bonds. I know that, even if we get lucky now, there would be no way to spend

the money – just save it so that I can start my own business when I get out of prison. With that in mind, gather the family members together and discuss which bond will be the most profitable to buy.

I have a request to make. Recently, I read in the prison newspaper *Hito [People]* that 'special brushes' to rub your body with are on sale. If you can get hold of one of them, could you bring it to me as a gift on your next visit? I have been giving myself a regular rubdown to keep healthy ever since I was on trial, but instead of towels, which might wear out, I am using stuff like floorcloths. This isn't very hygienic, that's why I'd like to ask you either for the special brushes or the loofah with strings attached that I was using back home. Please tell this to the officer in charge and ask for his permission. I'm sure he would say yes.

I don't have much time left to write, so let's discuss all other things when we meet.

But Shibata, who had been hardening himself in preparation for the day he got out of prison, fell ill at the end of 1944. On the door of his solitary cell, a sign saying 'Serve only rice porridge' was hung; after a few days it was changed to another sign that said 'Occupant is allowed to lie down'. Not long after I saw all this, Shibata disappeared quite suddenly from his solitary cell. Taguchi and I were both worried. Had he been transferred to another cell? Or because of his long sentence had he been sent out to work in another factory? Or another prison? Did it mean we wouldn't meet again?

One day after a month had passed, Shibata returned to his solitary cell. But he had contracted a serious illness. With such poor quality food everyone was malnourished. Once your sentence was determined and you were imprisoned, visitors were no longer allowed to bring you food and clothing.

Taguchi always called out as loudly as he could at roll call, trying to keep us aware of his existence and as an encouragement for Shibata.

It was a cold day at the end of November. Shibata, who never failed to miss exercise, did not come out. I worried that his illness had relapsed. Getting ill in prison was decisive. In the early stages your movements would become lethargic and then you would not able to attend the morning and evening exercise. After that your face would become swollen. That would mark the end of you.

On a night at the end of December, I heard a commotion outside so I looked out of the peephole. A stretcher was brought to Shibata's cell, taken inside, and then it left with Shibata on it. I tried to see his face from my small peephole, opening my eyes as wide as I could. But I could not see his face under the dim light. The stretcher was carried by two of the prisoners who were trusted by the guards. A guard closed the door of the cell, and then, as though it was a trivial task, he took out the tag with Shibata's number on it in an officious manner.

Everyday supplies and control over speech

Having started a war with all the countries surrounding it, it did not matter how many troops Japan sent to the front, there were never enough. In every single household, all able-bodied males were conscripted and sent to fight.[40]

Around this time my brother-in-law was conscripted, despite having five children and being over forty years old. Fortunately, since he was not sent outside Japan, he survived and returned without injury after the war. Anyone who wasn't conscripted was drafted into factories. But again it did not matter how many workers were drafted, the factories always suffered from labour shortages.

In each town, the neighbourhood associations increased their control over the population. All of life's necessities were rationed and savings were made compulsory. Precious metals had to be surrendered to the

---

40 Initially, first born or only sons and university students were exempt, but as the demand for recruits became more urgent all males over twenty were conscripted. This explains the high number of university students in the *kamikaze* units. Letters from many of them show that they were anti-imperialist or at least unconvinced of the aim of the war.

government. Even family heirlooms such as rings were taken.

People were constantly busy – sending soldiers off to the front, visiting families left behind to express sympathy, attending fire drills and bamboo spear training in preparation for the enemy landing in the country.

Those who had sorghum, rice and pressed wheat as their staple were lucky. People started receiving sweet potatoes, potatoes and eventually acorn flour as rations, which had been strictly reduced to 300 grams a day per person. The newspaper even began to run articles on various edible grasses. The monthly ration included less than 700 grams of miso paste and a mere 75 grams of vegetables; we received fish, mostly pollack, only occasionally. Sugar, cooking oil and clothes all required stamps.

As the air raids worsened, houses near railway lines were compulsorily demolished to minimise fire spreading as they were mostly wood and paper constructions. Children were evacuated in groups to the countryside.

In order to maximise public ignorance about the war situation, the government further increased its control over media and speech. Newspapers carried only announcements from the imperial headquarters, which were a pack of lies. Reporting on the damage inflicted on the US military, for example, was grossly exaggerated to about ten times the actual number, while the damage Japan suffered was reduced to one-fifth. As a result, the Japanese public had no idea about the real situation of the war. Nevertheless, because of phrases such as 'Death with honour' and 'Changing course' [withdrawal] appearing in the newspapers, the public, began to feel instinctively that something was wrong.

The USA then stepped up its counterattacks on Japan. In 1944 the Marshall Islands, Saipan and the Mariana Islands were all conquered. As the surrender of Saipan facilitated air raids on the Japanese mainland, Japan's main cities suffered air raids over many consecutive days. We prisoners knew little about this.

13
Death of Shibata in prison and the defeat

Losing two irreplaceable people

When I went out to exercise at the end of February 1945 I heard a rumour from one of the other prisoners that Japan was experiencing successive defeats at the front line. I let Taguchi know. Then, looking out from under his woven hat and, with eyes filled with tears and in a sorrowful voice, Taguchi said, 'Shibata is dead'. I felt as though all the blood in my body had drained away. After returning to my cell, I just wailed.

Japan's ruling class had taken away forever our precious mentor. If only he had held on for another six months he would have seen the defeat of Japan's militarism, been free and again stood at the forefront of the printworkers' struggle. But Shibata did not manage to see that day and died in prison. He was thirty-eight and had been single all his life.

His was a life given to the working class. Even during the war he continued, without wavering, to resist and oppose the regime. Shibata lived his whole life protecting the organisation of workers and assiduously nurturing many antiwar activists, a job that was made all the more difficult due to the repressive political and social conditions. Due to the ruling class's systematic social and political repression, the vanguard party, the JCP, which had flown the antiwar flag, was completely destroyed. All other antiwar activities were suppressed. For that reason Japan's resistance struggle was limited in the extreme. This is why the organisation Shibata had contributed to was so important. The Club was a way to continue working class activism as well as developing working class activists.

Conditions in the prison deteriorated. The number of guards continued to decrease. Mostly only higher ranks remained and they responded to the war conditions by becoming more and more irritated every day.

As a result of cold and malnourishment I had chilblains on the backs of both hands. As they were badly inflamed, I asked the guard doing the rounds for medicine. He yelled:

> You think I would give traitors like you fuckers any medicine? Even the soldiers on the front line don't have any medicine. The Americans will land in Japan any day now. Then I will kill you lot, and then we will die too. You are not going to need any damn medicine.

A prisoner trusted by the guards took us out for exercise, and spoke to us in an extremely unguarded manner:

> Hey guys, I heard that the warship *Musashi* was destroyed. That 7200 ton warship! I also heard that Saipan has fallen, so I would say that Taiwan and Okinawa will be taken pretty soon. I even heard that the Japanese combined fleet has totally disappeared somewhere. Tōjō's going to quit and that will be the end of Japan. You lot will be released then. Lucky fellows! I and my mates won't be so lucky though.

This was when I found out Tōjō was resigning [18 July 1944]. The continuing defeats, the worsening living standards and a country that was like scorched earth meant that the public lost confidence in him. Finally, the fall of Saipan seemed the right time for him to leave.

Nevertheless, despite having experienced a series of defeats, Japan saw itself as in too deep, with no longer any way back. People prayed for 'the divine wind [*kamikaze*] to blow again', but of course these prayers were never answered. Japan had to create the divine wind with its own hands. Those were the days when the government was trying to turn the tide of war with the *kamikaze*, which the Americans, out of fear and contempt, referred to as suicide bombers.

The US bombing of Japan intensified. The areas where members had been active, where there was a concentration of very small factories – Shiba, Kyōbashi, Kanda – were mostly reduced to ashes.

The largest factories in the printing industry were also hit. The Shitaya Factory owned by Toppan burned down in the air raid of 10 March. At the Itabashi Shimura Factory however, workers who remained to defend the factory fought hard to keep the fire damage to a minimum. While the B-29 fighter planes dropped incendiary shells like rain, these workers ran up and around the building with water pumps and buckets in their hands to quench the fire, giving preference to defending the factory and in so doing, sacrificing their own homes and furniture.

The same happened at Tokyo Shoseki. During the air raid of 13 April, a number of workers gathered at the factory and managed to protect it from fire using nothing more than water buckets, although everything else around the nearby station burnt to ashes. Kyōdō Printing was directly hit by bombs and burnt down completely. The Enokicho Factory owned by Greater Japan Printing was also destroyed. Tosho Printing (then Teikoku Printing) burnt down completely during the 25 May air raids. The workers fought hard to extinguish the fire but failed. When the morning came, they stood in a daze among the ruins of the fire. However, they soon mustered enough energy to pick up pieces of lead that could be used for casting type. The workers fought with all their might to protect the workshops where they made a living.

The day of the Great Tokyo Air Raid was 10 March [1945]. Because of the indiscriminate nature of the carpet bombing, on this one day alone 260,000 homes were burnt down and 100,000 people burnt to death. The damage was particularly severe in the downtown working class areas since they were full of wooden houses in close proximity to each other. Areas like Fukagawa and Honjō, where many Club members lived, including Shibata, Taguchi and me, were completely destroyed. Our homes were all burnt on this day.

My wife Nishida died in this bombing attack. Shibata's mother and sister and two of my sisters survived. Sakamura and Shiraishi rushed over to rescue them. They were taken in by Shiraishi's uncle, whose house was spared from the bombings. Shiraishi was also living with his uncle at the time. Later, my own two sisters were temporarily looked after by his uncle as well.

The number of bodies that were recovered and buried shows the extent of the damage from these raids. For example 13,000 bodies were buried in Kinshichō Park, 4900 in Sumida Park and 8400 in Ueno Park, all in Tokyo's working class areas.[41]

Mizuno was worried about everyone and went over to see them at Shiraishi's uncle's. Of course those of us in prison were completely unaware of any of this.

One day in April, I was called by the prison chaplain. Wearing a broad woven straw hat, I was taken by a guard and we headed towards the prison chapel. But our destination was a small building in front of the chapel. The chaplain told me to take a seat. When I took off my hat the chaplain said:

> I'd like to get to straight to the point, but it's extremely difficult news to convey. I was asked by your mother to tell you. On the 10 March Great Tokyo Air Raid, your wife was in the bombing and burnt to death. I heard that she tried to escape the bombing with her father but along the way they became separated. She took refuge in the local primary school but then the school was directly hit by bombs. Your mother was supposed to deliver this news to you, but she could not bring herself to do so. That is why she asked me to talk to you. We must accept this as a person's fate. Please don't lose strength and continue to take care of yourself. I only invited you over to tell you this.

I felt as though the blood had left my whole body and I was going to faint. I now knew the reason why letters from my wife had stopped. Only just the other day Shibata had died here in prison; this time my wife had died.

My wife, despite limited means, had given birth to our child during the war. In the midst of the fierce air raids, she raised our newborn child, all the

---

41 Shōwa 50 nen Shi (Fifty Years of Shōwa History) v4: 140.

while bringing gifts to me in prison, continuously encouraging me. Now the bombs had taken her away. The chaplain offered words of comfort to me, though I felt completely numb.

Thanking the chaplain I went out into the corridor. In order to hide my tears I quickly pulled down my woven hat. Walking behind the guard, the corridor seemed endless. The thing I remember to this day is that as I walked towards my solitary cell, the weather that day was beautifully sunny and that even in the midst of a war, the cherry blossoms in the prison garden were in full bloom.

Yokohama also experienced heavy air raid attacks and naval bombardment. May was a time of repeated air raids. The prison was full of detainees brought in from other police stations in the city to avoid the bombing. The sound of bombs was audible even in prison, and sometimes the door to my solitary cell was unlocked.

Release from prison

World War 2 was obviously nearing its end. Nio Jima, known in English as Iwo Jima, was captured [March 1945] and the US army arrived in Okinawa [April - June 1945]. Despite all this, Japan's military would not acknowledge defeat, proclaiming 'one billion should die in honour'. Aiming for the decisive battle on the mainland, the government even forced the public to train using bamboo spears.

Those of us in prison recognised the war situation and understood Japan was approaching defeat. However, the real situation was much worse than what we had heard. Japan was actually a mere step away from defeat.

At the beginning of this book I recounted how a number of political prisoners, including myself, faced Japan's day of defeat [15 August 1945] so I will not touch on that day here.

Every day I communicated via hand gestures with the man in the cell opposite me. When new prisoners arrived, we would receive new information. The trusted prisoner would not respond when we questioned him. We started getting treats for meals more frequently, but we were not allowed to go out for exercise. Boring days where we did nothing continued.

After two weeks, we were at last allowed to go out for exercise. The trusted prisoner was very talkative as he led us out to the exercise area.

> Guys, you can talk to whoever you like, because Japan has lost the war, you know. I was in Sakuragichō [in Yokohama] the other day, and there were a lot of American soldiers there. You should see the way all the girls have changed. No indigo pants suits any more; they're now wearing short skirts, so short that their behinds might show when they bend over. Oh, I just can't wait to be released!

He made us all laugh with such stories. He also criticised the prison guards, who at the time of the surrender, looted the prison supplies and took home rice, miso, clothes and medicines meant for prisoners. He said, 'I mean, they are the real thieves. I'm going to tell folks all about those shits when I get out'. I was suffering with scabies, but when I heard this I had confidence that I would get out.

I got my first letter in a long time from my younger sister. The letter said she had heard I was getting out and asked me to let her know the day of release as she would come and pick me up. But we had no idea about any of the details.

One day, those of us in solitary cells were gathered together in one place. We were given hemp ropes of very good quality that were used by the navy. The ropes were cut and unwound, and we learnt how to weave *zōri* using them. People began to guess that these sandals were for us to wear on our release, which greatly encouraged us. My heart filled with expectation, I made two pairs with great care.

The prison authorities however showed no sign of releasing us. We learnt that the ministries of justice and internal affairs had stated that they were not considering releasing political prisoners at all. Taguchi and I gradually succumbed to despair, resigning ourselves to the fact that we would have to serve the full sentence.

All the while the Allied forces steadily progressed with their rule over Japan.

But the day of our release, 6 October, did arrive. I was full of emotion.

Shibata and my wife came to my mind. My heart was full as I thought again if only he had lived another six months he could have been released with us.

That day, as Taguchi and I stood on the Yokohama station platform, we had close cropped hair, we were dressed in the same cotton summer kimono we had been wearing when we were arrested and held a cloth wrapped parcel under our arms. Whoever looked at us would know we were returning from prison. We were surprised by the American soldiers, white and Black, sitting on the station fence and chatting in loud voices, while in front of them, Japanese people were silently coming and going, wearing shabby military uniforms and all of them shouldering backpacks.

Taguchi and I got off the train at Yurakuchō station. We were then reunited with Taguchi's father. He was living at his house in Kyōbashi, which was spared from the bombings.

Four days later, on the 10 October, Tokuda Kyūichi, member of the JCP, and several other political prisoners were released from Fuchū prison. This was the moment when Japan's democratisation process took off.

The next day, I visited my younger sister in Funabashi and asked her the address of the farm in Chiba where my mother had been evacuated to. When I visited, my mother was well and in high spirits, much more so than I had expected.

A week later I somehow managed to buy a ticket to Shizuoka and boarded a train to visit my late wife's family home and to meet my only daughter. The train, which was so crowded that there was nowhere to sit, had broken windows and the majority of people on the train were either going to buy food or were black marketeers.

At my wife's family home her father apologised to me for letting his daughter die in my absence. Then he gave me my small daughter to hold.

I cried. Then I thought: Why couldn't we prevent the war even though we had trade unions in Japan?

14
The sown seeds bear fruit

Club members rise up

The ill-advised war was over. For the ruling class, it was a dark defeat, but for most of the working class, whose members had lived through the feudal times of the imperial system since the Meiji period, the end of the war meant liberation from tyranny. The public did not know what kind of fate lay ahead, but most were certain that it would be a brighter world where they could live humanely.

The world changed at a dizzying pace in the post-war peace. Japan was occupied by the Allied forces, in effect by the US army, and Japan's military was dismantled. We were released from prison because the Order Concerning Democratic Rights, introduced on 4 October, left the government no option but to release all political prisoners, including the communists. The Special Police, who had made our lives hell, was also abolished. Through this order, all the repressive laws that had limited freedom of ideology, speech, publishing and meetings, such as the Peace Preservation Law and the Military Secret Protections Act, were repealed.

Subsequent reforms focused on removing everything that had been a trigger to war. Business conglomerates were broken up, land reform implemented, separation of religion (Shintō) and state was announced, pre-war history, geography and morals textbooks were prohibited and militarists were banned from taking public office.

New laws guaranteeing the formation of unions and freedom of speech, publications and association were introduced as a result of democratic forces around the world uniting and utterly defeating the fascist countries, giving freedom to us in Japan.

All the Club members – those who had been imprisoned, those who had assisted the workers while looking after families suffering war damage, those who had been conscripted to fight at the front and those who had been mobilised as conscript labour – we all recognised that we now had two duties to fulfil.

The first was to rebuild the union movement. Before anything else we needed to bring printworkers together in a way that would continue the spirit of the NCTU in order to rebuild a national organisation with a class focus for each industry. The second, which could only be carried out by printworkers, was to set up a print works to produce newsletters for the JCP and other democratic organisations that would be the tools for Japan's democratisation. For this purpose, we needed as many progressive printworkers as we could gather.

As soon as I had made arrangements to bring my scattered family together, I went off to Taguchi's place in Kyōbashi. This area had a high concentration of smaller print works, so it was the perfect place to restart our activism.

It was here that one day we were reunited with Nakajima. He said to us: 'Thank you for all your efforts. I am so sorry that I was not able to do anything while you were away.' Actually, far from not doing anything Nakajima had continued to comfort the remaining families and maintained contact between people in our absence. Taguchi and I soon set about gathering the printworkers based in Kyōbashi. In addition, we visited the offices of the now legal JCP and both of us joined the party. By this time, the early stages of trade union formation had started in workplaces.

The painful war had ended but because the capitalists sabotaged production and created drastic inflation, most workers barely had enough to eat. Rice was rationed and the amounts available were impossible to sustain life. Workers had to run around everywhere just to buy enough food. But there was nothing for workers who, because of low wages, had no money. A worker from Toppan Printing said:

> I took the cotton out of my bedding and made a large padded kimono, I took that to a farmer's house and swapped it for rice. For three days I could give my child rice to eat.[42]

Life was so tough that many people were driven to become peddlers or black marketeers in order to eat. The price of goods shot up. Workers responded by rapidly forming trade unions, often spontaneously. Workers at Toppan Printing formed a union on 4 December 1945 in order to fight for wage increases. Workers in the Greater Japan Printing Company formed a union on 4 November 1945, and Toshō Printing formed theirs on 21 January 1946. It was clear that a national meeting of printworkers was needed.

On 27 January 1946 Taguchi and I attended the Kantō Area Factory Representatives Meeting as representatives of the Kyōbashi Medium, Small and Micro Sized Printworkers Union. There we met three representatives from the unions of the big printing companies. With the assistance of the Kantō Region Union Federation, we were able to speak openly about forming an industry-wide organisation of printworkers. The tide of democratisation was unbelievably strong and workers in many industries were forming industry-based unions. We agreed that we would similarly begin preparations to form an industry-wide printers union.

The preparatory committee met at the office of the Greater Japan Printing Union and decided that the union would be for printworkers as well as for those in publishing. Unions from the big publishing houses, such as Shufu no Tomo Sha [the company publishing the magazine Housewife's Friend], Iwanami Shōten, Tōhan and Nippan also participated on the committee. On 7 April 1946 the first national organisation for print and publishing workers, the All Japan Printing and Publishing Trade Union, formed; it represented 15,000 members.

---

42 Quote from *Toppan Rōdō Kumiai 10 nen Shi (Ten Year History of the Toppan Union)*. In the original quote it states the rice had been cooked and was hard. It is probable the rice had been cooked all at once to conserve fuel, but after three days without refrigeration, the rice had started to go hard. Given the scarcity of food and the effort required to obtain it, even hard rice would have been appreciated.

The first meeting was a grand affair. Taguchi was elected an executive committee member and I was elected as the permanent secretary. We had asked performers from the New Drama movement to perform a play based on the book that is the pride of all printworkers, *The Street Without Sunlight*, which is about the Kyōdō Print works struggle. But the performance did not happen as the delegates got overexcited and agreed to participate in the Give Us Rice Demonstration, which occurred at the same time. The play was cancelled at short notice, and I still feel bad about that for the actors.

Cooperating in the birth of the CIU

Soon after the union formed I was contacted by unions throughout the country. Many former Club members who left Tokyo to flee the war, were now standing up to form unions in their respective areas.

While preparing for the creation of the union we were also preparing for the formation of the Council of Industrial Unions (CIU), which would later play a central role in the post-war union movement throughout the whole of Japan. I also attended several preparatory meetings and cooperated in its formation.

In August 1946 the CIU was established with twenty-two member unions and 1,620,000 members. Immediately it embarked on a major struggle. The Print and Publishing Workers Union, whose members were at the CIU's core, responded to the fight against the sacking of national rail workers and seafarers. A general strike, centred in Tokyo, ensued around the demand for a unified union agreement. The strike was well organised and ended in victory. All the time, Taguchi and I ran around everywhere as activists, and worked hard to maintain contact with Club members.

Meanwhile, the rebuilt JCP was in desperate need of its own print works. Their pre-war newspaper, *Sekki*, was reissued after the war with the help of an external print works and called *Akahata*[43]. Under pressure from GHQ however, this print works was no longer willing to do it. The JCP leadership

---

[43] The name change reflects a different reading of the logographic Chinese characters in Japan's writing system known as Kanji. The English translation, *Red Flag*, remains the same.

then turned to Club members for help. Shiraishi, who was unemployed, happily took on this honourable task. With the participation of many other Club members, Shiraishi laid the basis for Hikari Printing, which would later become Akatsuki Printing. Soon many other democratic print works were established with the assistance of Club members.

Disregarding his own health, Shiraishi built the foundation for democratic print works throughout the country and trained a number of young printworkers to follow in his footsteps. He died on 8 November 1959 at the age of forty-eight.

What significance did the role carried out by Club members have in establishing democratic print works in Japan? In 1977 there was an unveiling ceremony of the commemorative stone monument dedicated to the Club. Watanabe Susumu, adviser to Akatsuki Printing commented:

> The Club holds a special place in the pre-war and post-war history of the immortal struggle of printworkers. Today, at the unveiling of this splendid monument commemorating the Club's struggle, I would like to convey my congratulations and heartfelt thanks on behalf of all class conscious and democratic print works.
>
> Today, there are 13 print workshops in total where most of the publications of unions and democratic organisations are done, including all the printed materials and magazines of the Japanese Communist Party. They are spread from Hokkaido [north] to Okinawa [south] and employ more than 15,000 workers. With more than 30 rotary press printing machines, among others, these workshops have all the equipment fit for a modern factory.
>
> Democratic print works like ours have seen huge progress in the last 30 years of the post-war period. That we could advance is due to the encouragement and support we have received from the JCP, the various unions and democratic organisations, but also because of the Club. It is because Club members, who kept alight the flame of the print and publishing workers' struggle, despite all the repression they

had to endure in the pre-war period, passed on their revolutionary tradition and the noble spirit of self-sacrifice to Hikari Printing. This in turn kindled the birth of democratic print works around the country.

We shall never forget how in the post-war period, Club members, of whom Taguchi and Sugiura are representative, poured all their energy into the union movement and how the late Shiraishi and others created Hikari Printing, from which Akatsuki Printing and other workshops followed. They dedicated their lives to guaranteeing that the publications and materials of the JCP and other democratic organisations are printed without fail.

If I may speak bluntly, it would not be an exaggeration to say that the national democratic print works were born and nurtured from Hikari Printing, growing to become this powerful single force today.

We faced indescribable difficulties during the establishment of the Hikari Printworks. Our success was due to the Club members who worked under these conditions without expecting to be repaid; instead, they silently picked the type, held the compositing stick, composed and distributed the type for *Akahata*. I started at Hikari Printworks in September 1946 as an apprentice and have worked until today, but those who have taught and guided me were those members of the Club.

Today, as we ponder the weight of responsibility and duty that has come to us, we must continue the tradition and revolutionary spirit of all those like Shiraishi and everyone from the Club. While resolving to struggle hard for the development and advancement of print works, I have confidence that this commemorative stone will always continue to convey this message to all our comrades.

On 19 February 1948, we commemorated the day of Shibata Ryūichirō's death. At the regular annual meeting of the Club members, I proposed we disband the organisation. I remember that the contents of the proposal contained the following:

> Now that a splendid industrial union, the All Japan Printing and Publishing Union, which Shibata and all of us had desired, has been formed, we do not want the existence of the Club to stand in the way. From now on, each of us shall make our own endeavours in our own fields and devote all our energy in keeping with the spirit of the Club.

This proposal was put to all the participants present, and then the Club was formally disbanded.

While all of Japan's trade unions were destroyed under the repression of war time fascism, the Club defended its organisation, saving from eradication the thread that would later bring about the print and publishing union. When *Zenin Sōren* [the National Federation of Printing and Publishing Industry Workers' Unions] created a photo collation entitled *Print and Publishing Workers Going Forward* for union members' education, it traced a 100 year long history of the print and publishing industry workers' unions, with the Club centrally located within it.

Afterword, February 1981

At the time of World War 2, Japan's imperial government and military completely repressed and destroyed Japan's militant unions. The leaders of the right wing unions took control and forced all others into cooperating with the war effort. Finally, all unions disbanded and workers and the public were forced to cooperate in the war, through the bureaucratic organisation PIA. In Japanese trade union history there is no evidence that there were any unions in this period.

But even in these conditions, print and publishing workers in Tokyo evaded the net of the Special Police, maintained their organisation and tenaciously continued their activism. Irrespective of how many times the leadership was repressed, and finally imprisoned, they continued the organisation into the post-war period. This book is a record of that struggle.

The reason I decided to write this book in 1981 is that the political and social situations of today seem similar to the days when Japan was about to plunge into war.

Today the ruling class is openly trying to drive working people to war again.

The USA is gradually increasing pressure upon Japan, urging the government to strengthen its military power. Under this pressure, we are witnessing unsubtle trends towards amending our pacifist constitution so that Japan can send its self-defence force overseas. The financial world, a significant sponsor of the Liberal Democratic Party (LDP), is coordinating its demands with those of the USA, arguing that Japan should lift its arms manufacture and export ban, increase its defence budgets, amend the constitution and consider instituting a conscription system. The current cabinet, led by Prime Minister Suzuki Zenkō has given in to this pressure. In spite of the economic crisis, defence was given a separate framework when the 1981 budget was prepared: all fighter planes of the self-defence force were equipped with anti-aircraft guided missiles, the main fleets were equipped with torpedoes. A large scale military exercise was deliberately performed on 15 August, the anniversary of Japan's surrender. Eighteen cabinet ministers and the prime minister himself, visited Yasukuni Shrine[44]. The minister of justice declared his opposition to the constitution, and resolutions in support of 'bettering' the constitution have, under the lead of LDP members, been adopted in local assemblies. In short, the country is heading straight towards militarism.

In a situation like this, our activities were class conscious but there were many individual participants who were not, though they were supporters. Among these were many who died during the struggle. These people are in our memories. To remember them and so as not to forget the achievements of the Club, with the support of former members and from all the print works, we erected a commemorative stone to *Shuppankō Kurabu* on 6 November 1977 at a temple near where Shibata and Shiraishi had lived for a long time. JCP chairman Nosaka Sanzō provided the calligraphy on the stone.

The inscription reads:

> In 1935 with the *Zenkyō* union's Shibata Ryūichirō and Shiraishi [Mitsuo] at its core, print and publishing workers established the Society. In 1937 it became the Club. In the midst of harsh wartime repression the Club had 1500 members in over 100 workshops. In 1940 most of Japan's unions were absorbed into the PIA but the Club resisted. Through covert activism it protected the livelihoods and rights of workers as well as carrying out anti war activities. In 1941 many were arrested by the Special Police and three were tortured

---

44 Visiting the shrine is a controversial practice because it is where Japan's war dead are interred.

and murdered. In February 1945, without recanting [his commitment to communism] Shibata died in prison. At the end of the war Club members formed the All Japan Printing and Publishing Workers Union and worked hard to establish democratic print works. In 1947, having achieved its purpose, the Club disbanded.

This memorial will exist forever. November 1977.

1935年元 全協労働組合柴田隆一郎、白石を中心に、印刷出版労働者の新陸を目的として和工会を設立、1937年出版工クラブに改組、戦時下弾圧の厳しい中で東京都内百余工場に1,500名の会員を組織す、1940年日本の労働組合はすべて官製組織産業報国会へ吸収さる、出版工クラブはこれに抗して非公然活動を通じ印刷出版労働者の生活と権利、戦争反対の闘いを展開、1941年特高警察に探知され多数逮捕、3名殺獄、1945年2月柴田は非転向のまま獄死。終戦後クラブ員は全日本印刷出版労働組合結成と、民主的印刷所の基を作るため努力、1947年出版工クラブはその任務を果たし解散す。

ここに を作り永く記録する。1977年十一月

Interview with Mr Masao Sugiura

Kaye Broadbent visited the author of this book, Mr Masao Sugiura, at his home in Funabashi in May 2016. He was then 102 years of age. The following is based on the interview that she conducted, which was transcribed into written Japanese by Hiroko Yuki and translated into English by Kaye Broadbent.

We members of the former Club wrote the first edition of this book in 1960 because we wanted to correct the view that Japan's unions did not exist during the war. After we wrote it, it was suggested we include more detail and publish it again and make it available for sale. That's why we published the second version.

It's a lie to say that there was no union movement in Japan during the war. We fought a war of resistance for ten years. Why does this lie persist? At the time the Japanese ruling class exerted extreme pressure on us. There were many books on Marxism published and for sale in bookshops. Buying and reading them was fine; however, forming a study group or taking collective action resulted in arrest. That was the atmosphere of the time.

After the Meiji Restoration [1868–1912], Japan's constitution was written with the role of the emperor at its core. The wealth in the country belonged to the emperor and this included the people as his servants. State policy focused on *fukoku kyōhei* [wealthy country, strong army] and the emperor's power was strengthened at the expense of ordinary people. With the march to war, draconian laws were introduced, such as the Peace Preservation Law in 1925. You could not criticise the imperial system, and capitalism and legislation became more repressive. This was the atmosphere we were fighting in.

Those who experienced the reality of oppression in 1930 remember how Japan suffered extreme economic crisis. Most workers, including ourselves, had received only six years of primary schooling. Only the imperial family, soldiers, police and public servants received the national pension. Ordinary people got nothing. At the time the poor were beggars – it was very sad; apart from begging, most people got nothing. We were active in this social environment.

The founder of the Club was Shibata Ryūichirō. Shibata was an executive member of the NCTU, which was Japan's branch of the Profintern. At the time the NCTU was under a hard line leadership and as a result split into moderate and hard line factions, which were severely criticised by the Profintern. This revealed the struggle to everyone.

There were also those like Shibata, who argued that the working class struggle had to develop. Shibata was employed as a temporary typesetter for books in a large printing company. He wanted to build an organisation as part of NCTU. He started to look around for people with similar views, finding first Fujimoto, and then Shiraishi. Together they started a magazine, *Ayumi*, to publish poetry, short verse and simple stories written by workers. The magazine was widely read.

The printing industry at the time was dominated by five major companies. There were also many small and medium sized companies located in the book selling district of Kanda, Tokyo, where the Club was based and was active. At the time the majority of printworkers were employed on a temporary basis and were generally not unionised. These were the workers who the Club organised.

Shibata and all comrades worked hard to organise the workers in the workplace but there were no jobs and the strike they launched over pay and conditions suffered defeat, which, in the highly militarised and repressive conditions of the time, was somewhat inevitable. Shibata gathered a group of activists from the strike, many of them acquaintances, because he was committed to taking action and because he recognised that the existing workplace union was of no assistance. We resolved to create our own organisation, the Society, which was the forerunner to the Club, and I was one of the activists present at that meeting.

We formed the Society with printworkers. In the printing industry there are different types of printers – for posters and billboards, flyers, for printing money, for books and for English language materials. There were initially about 100 people and thirty committed activists. We undertook a number of activities, but it was difficult to grow beyond 100 members so doubts about the direction and activities started to arise among the members. We realised we needed to learn more and that our current group was too narrow, so we focused on widening our circle. Shibata warned us to avoid union officials who were arrogant or boastful and instead to look to our workplaces. They were a great bunch of activists – very keen to study and learn in the fight for a better life for everyone.

In an environment of increasing repression, we held the official launch of the Club in 1937; 200 people attended.

Marx and Engels were widely read and popular in the student movement but we were advised not to associate with students or the intelligentsia. Instead, we were to look to our workplaces where people were pure, brave and have a hard life; they also had not received much education. So this was our focus and strategy in building the organisation.

We were an inclusive organisation and welcomed ordinary people. We organised hiking, beach trips, games like *shōgi* and *igo* and *haiku* groups. *Haiku* is a particular form of poetry that is attractive to printworkers who generally had more learning than most workers at the time because they needed to be able read the thousands of Japanese characters. Many were self-taught or learnt on the job.

Also, if there was a strike happening we would go and support it. We would go postering, which, at the time, was very dangerous. I was imprisoned for 29 days for postering.

Under Shibata's guidance we would go around the factories in the neighbourhood, supporting strikes and collecting money. In the course of these activities and gatherings we would talk to newer participants about books we had read, and recommend they read them. There was a lot of proletarian literature available that featured the lives of workers and workplace struggles such as *Tokunaga Sunao's Taiyō no Nai Machi* [*The Street without Sunlight*] and authors such as Kobayashi Takiji (for example, *Kanikōsen [The Crab Cannery Ship]*). Through these activities we were able to expand our organisation.

One element was education of the leadership. We would divide into groups of five or ten and hold study groups. It was quite difficult. I was leading one study group but I had completed only six years of primary education, so I asked a university student to help as a tutor.

The political atmosphere was tough at this time; Japan had invaded China and the suppression of political activity was intense. There was a police box on every corner and in the neighbourhood where we operated there was a police station. The police regularly patrolled the neighbourhood. It was the same throughout Japan, so conducting study groups was really difficult – even possession of the books we were reading would have meant arrest.

This kind of activity was criticised by people who had experienced the student movement or other struggles; we did not engage with them but instead focused on our workplaces. But gradually it became more difficult – more and more books were delivered to the police and there would be at least one person at meetings who was a member of the Special Police. Police repression became even more intense; often a cop was stationed in the doorway of every print workshop.

Eventually, we could not organise May Day. All political activity was suppressed by the government, so we formed the Club and organised picnics and other gatherings, including a major sporting event.

Some of our activities were sports groups, a cherry blossom viewing group, and haiku and literature groups. Drawing on competition between the factories, activists in the union movement could organise workers around, for example, baseball competitions, away from the eyes of the Special Police. If we went to the theatre we would sing popular songs of the day. In this way we tried to reach out to others in other factories. There was no other organisation like this.

From the time of the Manchurian Incident in 1931, the war situation deteriorated and domestically Japan became more militarised. The USA cut off access to oil so the government looked further south to Indonesia and other countries for resources. The government then declared every citizen a soldier and even mobilised men over 40 years of age.

In this atmosphere, the Club's activities declined, mostly because many of the leadership were conscripted. No matter how hard we persevered, our opportunities for activity shrank.

At first, when the government issued the order for unions to dissolve and join the government's PIA, we did not obey. Even during the war, we continued some level of organisation. In small to medium sized workplaces, unions had disappeared and employment conditions were severe. The PIA was really what was called a war education organisation. It did not benefit workers at all.

Even in those war time conditions, the Club was able to carry out some activities. As well-known labour movement activist and historian Shiota Shōbei said, 'Even during the war years, Japan's labour movement sowed seeds'. In looking at the activities of the Club I really feel that.

I continued Shibata's legacy into the NCTU by trying to rebuild militant union activism. This book was put together based on my recollections and those of about 36 others.

Shibata believed that it was important that workplaces be the foundation – this was where new activists, sprouts from the seeds we had sown, would emerge.

Glossary

Note: It is Japanese practice to list surnames first when giving full names; these are commonly used by people when referring to each other. Sometimes only the surnames of the people are mentioned in the original Japanese version and given names are not known. It is usual practice to attach the non-gender specific 'san' after a person's name – rather like Ms or Mr – but we have omitted this convention for the ease of English language readers. In the original text women were referred to by their single and their married names. Both names are given here to minimise confusion.

Ayumi title of publication of the literary circle which preceded the Japanese Language Materials Printworkers Society and the Publishing Workers Club.
All Japan Printing and Publishing Trade Union first national organisation for print and publishing workers.
Akahata (Red Flag) Japanese Communist Party's newspaper in the post-war period. The name change from the pre-war *Sekki* reflects a different reading of the same logographic Chinese characters used in the Japanese writing system (*kanji*).
Akatsuki Printing (*see* **Hikari Printing**).
Black Dragon formed in 1901 as a paramilitary, right wing ultra nationalist organisation whose goal was the elimination of communism.
Chiba city east of Tokyo.
CIU Council of Industrial Unions *(Sanbetsu Kaigi)*.
Club, The Print and Publishing Workers Club (*Shuppankō Kurabu*), formed out of

the Society of Japanese Language Materials Printworkers in 1937 when, under militarist repression, they changed the basis of operation due to increased pressure on trade union-like bodies.
Council, The *Zenhyō* (National Council of Trade Unions).
Dōmei Press official news agency of imperial government of Japan.
Fujisaka club activist, participated in the postwar creation of Akatsuki Printing.
Fukagawa working class suburb.
Fukui a representative of the joint organisation of thirty-five companies that was formed to support the Tokyo Printing striking workers.
Funabashi city east of Tokyo.
GFL General Federation of Labour (*Sōdōmei*).
GHQ General Headquarters, the name by which the occupation forces in Japan were generally known.
Ginza Tokyo shopping district.
Greater Japan Printing Company a large printing company.
Greater Japan Printing Union the trade union in the Greater Japan Printing Company.
Haiku Japanese poem in seventeen syllables made up of a 5–7–5 syllabic form and traditionally containing a reference to the season it's written in.
Hikari Printing (later Akatsuki Printing) print works established in the postwar period by former Club members and supporters.
Hongō area of Tokyo.
Igo a chess-like board game.
IRAA Imperial Rule Assistance Association (1940–45), created by prime minister Konoe Fumimaro; all political parties were to dissolve to form a one party state.
Iwanami Shōten publishing company.
Iwata central figure in the 1937 Yasuhisa strike.
JCP Japanese Communist Party formed in 1922, dissolved in 1924, revived in 1925 as a broader party; members faced constant police repression and mass arrests, and most of the leadership were in prison or in exile. Nosaka Sanzō fled to China and worked with the 8th Route Army. The party reformed in 1945 when the remaining leading members were released from prison.
JPP Japan Proletarian Party.
Kamikaze or divine wind was a term coined in 1274 after Kublai Khan's fleet was

destroyed by a typhoon, the kamikaze thus saving Japan's mainland from attack; later applied to the so-called suicide bombers.
Kanagawa city near Tokyo.
Kanda book publishing and printing district in Tokyo.
Kantō Publishing Union union covering permanent printworkers.
Kensēikai a workers' organisation formed in Greater Japan Printing Company.
Kinshichō former working class area of Tokyo.
Kobayashi Takiji author of proletarian novels such as *The Crab Cannery Ship*; murdered in prison by police.
Kōmiya activist in the Club.
Kuomintang China's National People's Party formed in 1911; led by Chiang Kai-shek during World War 2 and ruled China until 1949 when the Chinese Communist Party declared victory in the civil war.
Kwantung Army group inside Japan's imperial army; stronghold of the Imperial Way faction whose senior leaders advocated the overthrow of civilian government. With the foundation of Manchukuo in 1932 this group played a controlling role in the political administration and defence of the new state.
Kyōbashi area of Tokyo, centre of government, bureaucracy and office printing.
LDP Liberal Democratic Party a conservative political party formed from the merger of conservative parties in 1955.
Meibunsha print shop set up in 1941 by core Club activists.
Mizuno Shizue activist in the Club's Women's Section; participated in the setting up of Akatsuki Printing.
Nabeyama Sadachika senior leader of the JCP; imprisoned during the war, recanted communist beliefs in prison.
Nadeshiko Mustumi Kai (Nadeshiko Friendship Association) women's group formed from the Club's Women's Section after the Club was ordered to dissolve.
Nakajima Club activist; postwar was JCP Tokyo central district committee member.
NCTU National Conference of Trade Unions (*Zenkyō*) JCP affiliated federation formed in 1928; in 1932 it had 16,000 members about half of whom were Korean labourers, as well as a proportion of day labourers.
Nippan publishing company.
Nishida Tomiko activist in the Club's Women's Section.
Nishio Suehiro secretary-general of the GFL.

Nomiya Eitarō member of the JCP during the war; murdered in prison by police.

PPL Peace Preservation Law 1925–45.

PIA Patriotic Industrial Association *(Sangyō Hōkoku Kai)*, formed in 1940 as a national organisation under the jurisdiction of the welfare ministry to mobilise and control labour.

Print Labour Club the Club's baseball team.

Profintern Red International of Labour Unions (1921–37), set up by the Comintern (Third International) as a rival to the International Federation of Trade Unions of the Second International.

Rakugo comedic storytelling.

Sakamura one of the first people Shibata Ryūichirō approached to form a literary circle.

Sakurai core activist in Shiba branch of the Society; active post-war in the Akatsuki Printworks.

Sakurai (née Yoshimura) activist in the Club's Women's Section.

Sano Manabu senior leader of the JCP; imprisoned during the war, recanted communist views in prison.

Sekiguchi member of the Club; postwar participated in creation of Akatsuki Printworks.

Sekki *(Red Flag)* title of the Japanese Communist Party's paper in the pre-war period. The name change to *Akahata* reflects a different reading of the same logographic Chinese characters used in the Japanese writing system (*kanji*).

Shibata Ryūichirō Club guide and mentor; died in prison.

Shibata Ichirō friend of Sugiura Masao and Shibata Ryūichirō.

Shiba main location for newspaper, money and industrial magazine printing.

Shinbashi former working class area of Tokyo.

Shiobara employed at Tokyo Printing but lost his job during the 1935 Tokyo Printing strike.

Shiraishi Mitsuo one of the first people Shibata Ryūichirō approached to form a literary circle.

Shiraishi Sei (née Watanabe) printworker; active in the Club's Women's Section.

Shizuoka city south of Tokyo.

Shōgi a chess-like board game.

Shuppankō Kurabu Print and Publishing Workers Club (*see* **the Club**).

Social Masses Party anti-capitalist, anti-fascist and anti-communist party; operated 1932–40.
Society, The Society of Japanese Language Materials Printworkers (*Wakōkai*). Formed in 1935 after the Tokyo printworkers strike; changed basis of its operations in 1937 when it became the Print and Publishing Workers Club.
Sōhyō Nihon Rōdō Kumiai Sōhyōgikai (General Council of Trade Unions) peak union organisation formed in 1950 as an anti-communist alternative to the powerful Council of Industrial Unions; in 1989 elected to dissolve and merge with the private sector-dominated *Rengō* (Japanese Trade Union Confederation).
Taguchi core activist in the Club; imprisoned with Sugiura Masao and Shibata Ryūichirō.
Takanashi Shigeharu communist, Club activist; believed preparation must be made for an armed insurrection in the Hiratsuka area (Kanagawa, south of Tokyo).
Takatsu Masao official of Kantō Publishing Union; postwar Japan Socialist Party parliamentarian.
Tōhan publishing company.
Tōjō Hideki general in the Japanese Army who was prime minister for much of the war; best known for ordering the attack on Pearl Harbour.
Tokyo Printing one of Tokyo's largest print works.
Toppan Printing a large printing company.
Toshō Printing a large printing company.
Tsujiki Small Theatre part of the New Drama movement; initially, the term was used to distinguish new theatrical experimentation from *kabuki*; gradually came to refer to specific theatre troupes that emerged in the early twentieth century. Today the term also refers to those troupes who trace their artistic lineage to their early troupes, the plays performed and their understanding of what theatre represents.
Wakōkai Japanese Language Materials Printworkers Society (*see* **the Society**)
Wakō no Tomo Friends of Printworkers of Japanese Language Materials, publication of the Society.
Worker–Farmer Faction later the Japan Proletarian Party, faction formed by Yamakawa Hitoshi who left the JCP because he disagreed with the Comintern's line and its control of the JCP.
Yagi Ito activist in the Club's Women's Section; postwar chair of a union's women's department.

Yamanashi Club activist responsible for liaising with police.

Yamato Nadeshiko term used to describe a Japanese woman who has all the traditional feminine graces and is the epitome of Japanese womanhood. *Yamato* is the ancient name for Japan and a *nadeshiko* is a type of carnation.

Yamazaki member of JCP.

Yuga member of JCP.

Yasukuni Shrine Japanese shrine where war dead are interred.

Yotsuya an area of Tokyo.

Zenin Sōren (National Federation of Printing and Publishing Industry Workers' Unions).

Zōri straw sandals.

Bibliography

References in the second Japanese edition 1981

Nihon Rōdō Kumiai Monogatari (The Story of Japan's Union Movement). n.d. Tokyo: Chikuma Shōbo.

The Committee Publishing the Writings of Shiraishi Mitsuo n.d. Akahata to Tomo ni (Together with Red Flag).

Document. n.d. Shōwa 50 nen Shi v4 (Fifty Years of Shōwa History v4). Tokyo: Shiobunsha.

Gendaishi Shiryō no.15 Shakaishugi Undō (Modern History Notes no.15 Socialist Movements).

Kindai Nihon Rōdōsha Undō Shi (The History of Japan's Modern Union Movement).

Naimūshō Keihō Kyoku edition (Ministry of Internal Affairs, Police Bureau). Shakai Undō no Jōkyō 1942 (The State of Social Movements 1942) v13. Tokyo: Sanichi Shōbo.

Naimūshō Keihō Kyoku edition (Ministry of Internal Affairs, Police Bureau). Shakai Undō no Jōkyō 1942 (The State of Social Movements 1942). v14. Tokyo: Sanichi Shōbo.

Ohara Social Science Institute. 1965. Taiheiyō Sensōka no Rōdō Undō (The Union Movement During the Pacific War). Tokyo: Rōdō Junpōsha.

Rekishi Kenkyūkai (ed). 1953. Taiheiyō Sensō Shi (A History of the Pacific War). Tokyo: Toyō Keizai Shinpōsha.

Shioda, S. 1982. Nihon Shakai Undō Shi. Tokyo: Iwanami Zenshō.

Social Masses Party. 1937. Shadaitō Senjika Undō Hōshin (1937 Social Masses Party Direction of the Movement During the War).

Tamiya, S. (ed). 1948. *Sekai Minshū Kakumei Nenpyō* (Yearbook of World Democratic Revolutions). Tokyo: Minshū Hyōronsha.*

Toppan Union. *Toppan Rōdō Kumiai 10 nen Shi (Ten Year History of the Toppan Union)*. Tokyo: Toppan Union.

Additional references used in the present English language edition

Banno, J. 2014. *Japan's Modern History, 1857–1937*. Routledge: London.

Broadbent, K. and O'Lincoln, T. 2015. 'Japan: Against the regime'. In D. Gluckstein (ed.). *Fighting On All Fronts: Popular resistance in the second world war*. London: Bookmarks.

Dower, J. 1993. *Japan in War and Peace: Essays on history, race and culture*. London: HarperCollins.

Finn, R. 1992. *Winners in Peace: MacArthur, Yoshida and postwar Japan*. Berkeley: University of California Press.

Fujihara, A. 1975. *Nihon Minshū no Rekishi 9: Sensō to Minshū* (Japan's History of Democracy 9: War and Democracy). Tokyo: Sanseido.

Gordon, A. 1991. *Labor and Imperial Democracy in Prewar Japan*. Berkeley: University of California Press.

Hane, M. 2000. *Japan: A short history*. Oxford: Oneworld Publications.

Ienaga, S. 1979. *Japan's Last War: World War II and the Japanese 1931–4*. Canberra: Australian National University Press.

Mitchell, R. 1992. *Janus-faced Justice: Political criminals in Imperial Japan*. Honolulu: University of Hawai'i Press.

Moore, J. 1983. *Japanese Workers and the Struggle for Power, 1945–1947*. Madison: University of Wisconsin Press.

Morris-Suzuki, T. 1984: *Shōwa: An Inside History of Hirohito's Japan*. Melbourne: Methuen.

Nimura, K. 1994. 'Post second world war labour relations in Japan'. In J. Hagan and A. Wells (eds). *Industrial Relations in Australia and Japan*. Sydney: Allen & Unwin.

Ohara Social Science Institute. 1965. *Taiheiyō Sensōka no Rōdō Undō (The Union Movement During the Pacific War)*. Tokyo: Rōdō Junpōsha.

---

* Every attempt was made by the translator to determine the correct edition of this book. The cited edition is most likely to be the correct one.

www.ingramcontent.com/pod-product-compliance
Lightning Source LLC
Chambersburg PA
CBHW070737020526
44118CB00035B/1404